the *Friendship* of Salem, Mass.

SUMATRAN PIRATES
AND
THE FRIENDSHIP

A NARRATIVE OF THE PIRACY, AND PLUNDER OF THE SHIP FRIENDSHIP, OF SALEM, ON THE WEST COAST OF SUMATRA, IN FEBRUARY 1831, AND THE MASSACRE OF PART OF HER CREW: ALSO, HER RE-CAPTURE OUT OF THE HANDS OF THE MALAY PIRATES (1831)

by

Charles M. Endicott

GENERAL INSTRUCTIONS TO COMMODORE JOHN DOWNES OF THE FRIGATE POTOMAC, *AND INSTRUCTIONS TO SEEK REDRESS FOR THE DESTRUCTION OF THE SHIP FRIENDSHIP, AT QUALLAH BATOO, ISLAND OF SUMATRA, AND HIS REPORT RELATIVE TO THE DESTRUCTION OF THE TOWN OF QUALLAH BATOO. (1832)*

from

Levi Woodbury, Secretary of the Navy

SICPRESS 2013
METHUEN, MASS.

Narrative of the piracy and plunder of the Ship Friendship, of Salem, on the west coast of Sumatra, in February, 1831; and the massacre of part of her crew, also her recapture out of the hands of the Malay pirates by Charles M. Endicott, was originally read before a meeting of the Essex Institute January 28, 1858 and published in 1959 at Salem, Mass. A version of this account was published in *the Boston Courier* by the author of this account; in the summer of 1852.

General Instructions To Commodore John Downes, Of The Frigate Potomac, And Instructions To Seek Redress For The Destruction Of The Ship Friendship, At Quallah Batoo, Island Of Sumatra, And His Report Relative To The Destruction Of The Town Of Quallah Batoo provided by Levi Woodbury, Secretary of the Navy, is found in the *American State Papers, Documents, Legislative And Executive, of The Congress Of The United States, from The Second Session of The Twenty-First To The First Session of The Twenty-Forth Congress, Commencing March 1, 1831, and Ending June 15, 1836: Class VI. Naval Affairs, Volume IV, 1861.*

©2013
SicPress.com
14 Pleasant St.
Methuen, Massachusetts.
sales@sicpress.com

TABLE OF CONTENTS

Introduction 7

Sumatran Pirates and the Friendship *A Narrative of the piracy and plunder of the Ship Friendship, of Salem, on the west coast of Sumatra, in February, 1831; and the massacre of part of her crew, also her recapture out of the hands of the Malay pirates*.... 9

General Instructions To Commodore John Downes, Of The Frigate Potomac, *And instructions to seek redress for the destruction of the Ship Friendship, at Quallah Batoo, island of Sumatra, and his report relative to the destruction of the town of Quallah Batoo.* 47

Index 77

NARRATIVE

OF THE

PIRACY AND PLUNDER

OF THE

SHIP FRIENDSHIP, OF SALEM,

ON THE

WEST COAST OF SUMATRA,

IN FEBRUARY, 1831;

AND THE MASSACRE OF PART OF HER CREW; ALSO, HER RECAPTURE OUT OF THE HANDS OF THE MALAY PIRATES.

BY CHARLES M. ENDICOTT.

[FROM THE HISTORICAL COLLECTIONS OF THE ESSEX INSTITUTE.]

SALEM:
Printed at the Gazette Office, for the Essex Institute.
1859.

INTRODUCTION

Charles Moses Endicott (1793-1863), the son of Moses (a shipmaster who died in Havana in 1807) and Anna Towne, was educated at Phillips Academy in Andover. By fifteen he was working in the Salem counting house of his uncle. For fifteen years following the War of 1812, Endicott traded along the Sumatra coast, being engaged chiefly in the importation of pepper. His survey of the treacherous Sumatran coastline, (*Sailing Directions for the Pepper Ports on the West Coast of Sumatra* published in 1833), was widely used, including by the United States Navy.

The pepper trade was extremely lucrative and extremely dangerous. In the years between 1799 and 1846, 179 ships sailed between Salem and Sumatra. The pepper ports known to the Salem merchants - Qualah Batoo (now Kuala Batee), Muckie, Soosoo, Pulo Kio - are located in what is now known as the Aceh Province in Indonesia.

The natives were often hostile and extremely eager to capture American ships, killing crew members and plundering their cargo while ships lay in port. The actual trading of pepper occurred on dry land--the captain and a couple of crew members would go ashore, exacerbating the risk of midnight raids by pirates. Captains were sometimes captured while trading onshore and held for ransom by the local chieftans, however, to Salem Captains, the rewards outweighed the risks.

Captain Endicott commanded the Friendship, and a crew of seventeen, when it arrived at Pulo Kio in 1831. Awakened in the middle of the night by the watch, a small boat approached the ship. The crew prepared to board the smaller boat to determine whether or not their story was true. Although they really did have pepper on board the smaller ship, Endicott immediately suspected it had been sent to test their watch.

When the new crop of pepper was ready, Po Adam, a local dignitary and a friend of the Salem merchants expressed fears for the safety of the ship. When Endicott went ashore at Qualah Batoo to trade, he impressed on his crew the need for extreme viligance.

While the natives on shore were suspiciously slowly bringing Endicott the bags of pepper one by one-the ship was violently taken by a boatload of pirates. Endicott and the men who had accompanied him on shore barely escaped with their lives.

Using a small boat, they reached the safety of the port of Muckie, where lay the brigs *Governor Endicott* of Salem, and *the Palmer* of Boston and the ship *James Monroe* of New York. The three ships retook the Friendship by force. After an armed battle, the pirates abandoned the thoroughly looted the Friendship. In the end five men of *the Friendship* had been killed and six injured.

In retribution, President Andrew Jackson sent *the US Frigate Potomac* to Quallah Batoo on February 7th, 1832, destroying the nearby forts and engaging in hand to hand combat. Over 150 of the Malay pirates, including their local chieftan were killed in attacks. On February 9th, the men returned to the *Potomac* and the vessel proceeded to bombard the village itself, its cannons setting fire to and destroying the village - and killing over 300 of its inhabitants.

Sumatran Pirates and the Friendship
Narrative of the piracy and plunder of the Ship Friendship, of Salem, on the west coast of Sumatra, in February, 1831; and the massacre of part of her crew, also her recapture out of the hands of the Malay pirates

Before proceeding with the narrative, I will say a few words upon the character of the natives of this coast; the impression having gone abroad, and has even been stated in our pulpits and elsewhere, that the wrongs they have experienced at our hands have led to their bad faith and perfidy; and that we. Americans, are, after all, responsible for it. That this is a base calumny and has no foundation in truth, we shall first endeavor to show.

It may be proper perhaps to state in the outset, that the whole of the pepper coast is inhabited by emigrants from Acheen, the residence of the king, and the capital of his dominions; and although they are generally spoken of by us as Malays, are nevertheless a distinct race from them, speaking an unwritten language wholly unlike the Malay tongue and differing from them in everything but their religion. The Acheenise have an imperfect and vague tradition, which savors more of fable than reality, that they are the descendants of a people, who, at a very remote period, emigrated from the Mediterranean, or, as they express it, from "Roma," (by which is meant, no doubt, a colony of Phoenicians,) who, in the course of their extensive maritime enterprises, visited the northern part of this island by way of the Red Sea, and formed a settlement at Acheen, where intermarrying with the natives their posterity have ever since resided.

The coast from Acheen southward was originally peopled by Malays, but wherever the Acheenise have made settlements the aborigines have invariably been exterminated, either by secret assassination or poison: and by such and kindred foul practices they have possessed themselves of the whole of the pepper coast, and scarcely a real native Malay is now met with. All writers, for centuries past, have agreed in representing these people as the most subtle, crafty and treacherous of all the nations of the East. Our dealings with them generally (I will not say always—for bad and unprincipled men are sometimes found engaged in all trades,) but generally our dealings with them are such as of necessity they must be with a people from whom we can never obtain redress for any bad faith or dishonesty; who acknowledge no laws, have no tribunals of justice to which we can appeal for broken faith or violated contracts, and hold themselves bound by no ties of integrity or honor; for it would be as difficult to carry out equitably any compact made with them if it should conflict with their interests, as it would be vain to expect mercy from the ferocious tenants of their forests. That they have at times been over-reached at their own play in their attempts to defraud and impose upon us, and that the measure they mete unto others has been measured to them again, will not be denied; and that our interests have also frequently suffered severely by their fraudulent practices, is equally certain. If we were not always on the alert to detect and counterbalance their frauds, and sometimes even to anticipate them, we should be obliged to abandon the trade altogether. But the Munchausen[1] stories which are sometimes banded about, are often without any foundation in truth, and are not unfrequently the offspring of the brain of individuals, who hope to gain in this way a character for great shrewdness in their dealings. But these trials at circumvention, in which they as often gain the advantage as lose it, do not certainly justify the piracy and murder of our countrymen trading upon their shores.

So far from becoming corrupt, perfidious and treacherous, by our intercourse with them, it will be found, by a little research, that these attributes in their characters existed, in as

[1] *outrageously farfetched stories*

eminent a degree, upwards of two centuries ago, as at present; and setting aside the insignificance into which the king's power has dwindled, the accounts of them then would answer as well as any description which could now be given. In Mayor's historical account of early voyages, is one of Commodore Bieulieu's to the East Indies in 1619-22, undertaken for commercial purposes, under the auspices of the French government. Mons. Bieulieu is represented as an officer of distinguished character, both for the integrity of his conduct and the extent of his abilities. The account he has given of his enterprise is universally admired, for candid statement, and easy, unaffected detail. He left France in October 2, 1619, with three vessels under his command, and in the course of his voyage visited Acheen, to obtain the king's permission to traffic within its dominions, he describes his reception by the king, and the pomp and magnificence of his court at that time, and also details several instances of his majesty's savage cruelty in mutilating his subjects upon the most trifling pretext, to which he was a painful eye-witness. Finally, after along negotiation, and submitting to much extortion, he succeeded in obtaining the desired permission, and, in his first attempts to avail himself of it, he gives the following account:

"The avarice of this monarch was not less detestable than his cruelty. No representations or presents could get the better of it. Notwithstanding I had procured a license to purchase pepper of his subjects, the first person who sold me any was laid in irons. At last I found it impossible to procure a grain, unless I consented to take it of him at his own price; and after I had agreed for three hundred bahars, at nearly double its value, to my astonishment, I found he exacted seven per cent, by way of custom, for the very pepper I had purchased of himself. I afterwards contracted with a person who was distinguished for his knowledge of the laws of Mahomet, and even passed for a prophet himself, but finding some black sand among his pepper, I remonstrated. At last I found he weighed out the commodity wet and although a complaint to the king might have procured me revenge, I chose rather to submit to the loss than enter into a dispute with this sanctified personage. Wearied out at length with the impositions of the tyrant and disgusted with the chicanery of his subjects, I resolved to depart."

This author also adds, "The inhabitants of Acheen are the most vicious of any on the coast. They are proud, perfidious and envious. With an outward show of being strict Mahometans, they are the most consummate hypocrites. If they only suspect that any one bears them any ill will, they endeavor to ruin him by false accusations."

Commodore Bieulieu's account is corroborated by all the early English navigators, who visited Acheen under the direction of the East India Company, immediately after its first charter by Queen Elizabeth in 1600. The character of these people, since that period, has undergone no radical or material change; it is essentially the same in all respects, now as then. We omitted to remark that Commodore Bieulieu had one of the vessels under his command burnt by the natives, and all the plunder detained by the king. We think no candid, liberal and unprejudiced mind will seek far, or look deep, for motives to stimulate such a mercenary people to acts of violence on our ships whenever opportunities offer; and that no other incentives are needed than such as are found inherent in their own breasts, that is, a love of plunder, to deeds of crime and outrage.

This, let it be borne in mind, was their character in the year 1620, the very year of the landing of the Pilgrim Fathers, at Plymouth. One can therefore appreciate how far we, Americans, who had then no existence as a nation, and who had no intercourse with these people for 170 years after this period, are responsible for these traits of character, and how far we therefore have corrupted their integrity. Having now finished our preface, we will commence our narrative.

And here we would remark, in compiling this account, we have met with a serious obstacle, which has baffled all our skill to overcome—that is, how to avoid the too frequent and objectionable use of the little personal pronoun I, which must strike every reader of the narrative, in common with myself. We trust, however, the peculiar circumstances of the case will be considered and appreciated, and that charity extended to me which the subject seems imperatively to demand.

The ship *Friendship*, of this place, under my command, belonging to the Messrs. Pickman and Silsbee, sailed from Salem for the west coast of Sumatra, with a crew of seventeen men, including officers and seamen, on the 26th of May, 1830. The persons composing the ship's company, were as follows: Charles M. Endicott, Master; Charles Knight, 1st Mate; John Barry, 2d Mate; William Bray, Carpenter; George Chester, Algernon Warren, John Davis, John Massey, George Collins, William Parnell, Gregorie Pedechio, Charles Converse, Philip Manning, John Patterson and John Byrne, Seamen; William Francis, Steward; Lorenzo Migell, Cook; and after the usual succession of fair winds and foul, calms and storms, arrived safely at her place of destination on the 22d September[1] following. We touched first at the port of Quallah Batoo*, in Lat. 3° 48' N. This place is inhabited by natives from the Pedir Coast, on the north of the island, as well as Acheenise, and 19 therefore governed jointly by a Pedir and Acheenise Rajah. We remained here for the purposes of trade, until the 5th of November following, at which time, having obtained all the pepper of the old crop, and the new pepper not coming in until March or April, we left that port, and m prosecution of our voyage visited several others, and finally returned to Pulo Kio[2], about two miles from Quallah Batoo, the latter part of January, 1831, intending to remain there until the coming in of the pepper crop.

One bright moonlight night, shortly after our arrival at this place, I was awakened by the watch informing me that a native boat was approaching the ship in a very stealthy manner, and under suspicious circumstances. I immediately repaired on deck,

[1] *in English, Rocky River*
[2] *in English, Wood Island,*

and saw the boat directly in our wake under the stern, the most obvious way to conceal herself from our observation, and gradually approaching us with the utmost caution, without the least noise or apparent propelling power, the oars being struck so lightly in the water that its surface was scarcely ruffled. Having watched their proceedings a few minutes, we became convinced it was a reconnoitering party, sent to ascertain how good a lookout was kept on board the ship, and intending to surprise us for no good purpose, to say the least, if they were not discovered. We therefore hailed them in their own dialect, asking them where they came from, what they wanted, and why they were approaching the ship in such a stealthy, tiger-like manner. We could see that all was instantly life and animation on board her, and after a few moments we received an answer that they were friends from Quallah Batoo, with a load of smuggled pepper, which they were desirous to dispose of to us. We however, positively forbade them to advance any nearer the ship, or to come along side; but, after considerable discussion, we at length gave our consent for them to come abreast the ship at a respectful distance, and we would send some of our own men on board to ascertain if their story was correct; and if there was nothing suspicious about her, on their giving up their side arms we would rig a whip upon the main yard, and in this way take on board their pepper, and allow one man to come on board ship to look after it. All our own crew had, in the meantime, been mustered and armed, and a portion of them placed as sentinels on each side the gangway. In this manner we passed on board some 50 or 60 bags of pepper. We were afterwards informed by the 2d officer that while this was going forward, the chief officer, who subsequently lost his life, was secretly scoffing at these precautions, attributing them to cowardice, and boasting he could clear the decks of a hundred such fellows with a single handspike. This boat, we subsequently ascertained, was sent by a young man named Po Quallah, the son of the Pedir Rajah, for the express purpose which we had suspected; the pepper having been put on board merely as an excuse in case they should be discovered. It was only a sort of parachute, let off to see from what quarter the wind blew, as a guide in their future evil designs upon us. Ascertaining, however, by this artifice, that the ship was too vigilantly guarded, at least, in the night, to be thus surprised, they set themselves at work to devise another plan to decoy us to Quallah Batoo, in which, I am sorry to say, they were more successful.

A few days after this occurrence, a deputation was sent to invite us to Quallah Batoo, representing that the new crop of pepper was beginning to make its appearance, and they could now furnish us with from one to two hundred bags per day, and would no doubt be enabled to complete loading the ship in the course of forty days. Being in pursuit of a cargo, and having been always on friendly terms with the natives of this place, who I did not consider worse than those of other parts of the coast, and feeling beside some security from the fact that we had already been warned by some of our old friends not to place too much confidence in any of them, all of whom, in consequence of the low price of pepper, and from various other causes, were actually contemplating piracy along the whole coast, whenever a good opportunity should offer, we considered, with a suitable degree of caution, the danger was but trifling, and therefore concluded a contract with them, and proceeded at once with the ship to Quallah Batoo. Strict regulations were then established for the securty and protection of the ship. Two of the most important were, that, in the absence of the captain, not more than two Malaya were to be permitted on board at the same time; and no boats should be allowed to approach her in the night time upon any pretense whatever, without calling an officer. Then mustering all hands upon the quarter deck, I made a few remarks, acquainting them with my apprehensions, and impressing on their minds the importance of a good look-out, particularly in the night, and expressed my firm conviction that vigilance alone would prevent the surprise and capture of the ship, and the sacrifice of all our lives; that the words of Po Adam, which they had so often heard him utter, "must look sharp," had no idle meaning. Having thus done all we could to guard against surprise, and put the ship in as good a state of defense as under the circumstances was possible; keeping her entire armament in good and efficient order, and firing every night an eight o' block gun, to apprise the natives that we were not sleeping upon our posts, we commenced taking in pepper, and so continued for three or four days, the Malays appearing very friendly, and everything went on satisfactorily.

On Monday, February 7, 1831, early in the morning, while we were at breakfast, my old and tried friend, Po Adam, a native well known to traders on this coast, came on board in a small canoe from his residence at Pulo Kio, in order to proceed on shore in the ship's boat, which shortly after started with the 2d officer, four seamen and myself. On our way Po Adam expressed much anxiety for the safety of the ship, and also an entire want of confidence in Mr. Knight, the first officer, which, however, I then considered unfounded, remarking in his broken English, "He no look sharp, no understand Malay-man." On being asked if he really believed his countrymen would dare to attack the ship, he replied in the affirmative. I then observed to the 2d officer, it certainly behooved us, the boat's crew, who were more exposed than any of the ship's company, to be on our guard against surprise, and proposed when we next came on shore, to come prepared to defend ourselves; but did not think the danger sufficiently imminent to return to the ship for that purpose at the present moment. When we reached the landing we were kindly received, as usual,—a man who was a stranger to me, of rather prepossessing appearance, pretended to be very much pleased with my knowledge of the language, for which he was profuse in his compliments, and, to hear me speak it, followed close upon my footsteps through the bazars, and was very assiduous in his attentions.—Such circumstances being, however, of almost daily occurrence, there was nothing particular in this to excite suspicions of any evil intent, and we were soon upon easy and familiar terms. The natives were bringing in pepper very slowly; only now and then a single Malay would make his appearance with a bag upon his head, and it was not until nearly 3 o'clock in the afternoon that sufficient was collected to commence weighing; and between three and four o'clock the first boat started from the shore. The natives were, however, still bringing in pepper, with a promise of another boatload during the day. This was, however, a mere subterfuge to keep us on shore. As the boat was passing out of the river, I noticed her stop upon one of the points, and believing it the; object of her crew to steal pepper, and secrete it among the neighboring high glass, two men were sent down to look after them. They soon returned, remarking there appeared to be nothing wrong. The ship lay about three fourths of a mile from the shore, and between the scale-house and the beach there was a piece of rising ground, so that standing at the scales we could just see the ship's topgallant yards. I had observed a vessel in the offing in the course of the day, apparently approaching this place or Soosoo, and, being at leisure, walked up towards the beach to ascertain if she had hoisted any national colors. The instant I had proceeded far enough to see our ship's hull, I observed the pepper-boat, which was at this time within two or three hundred feet of her, as she rose on the top of the swell, appeared to have a large number of men in her. My suspicions were instantly aroused that there was something wrong, and I returned to inquire into the circumstance of the men who were sent down to the mouth of the river. I was then informed, for the first time, as they approached the boat, six or seven Malays jumped up from the high grass and rushed on board her; and as she passed out of the river, they saw her take in from a ferry boat, that was passing, about the same number; but as they all appeared to be "youngsters," to use their own expression, they did not think the circumstance of sufficient importance to mention it. They were reprimanded for such an omission of duty, accompanied with the remark, "your youngsters, as you call them, will, I suspect, be found old enough in iniquity, at least, to capture the ship, if once admitted upon her decks." The words of Po Adam, that morning, that "Mr. Knight no look sharp, no understand Malay-man," now struck me with their full force and a fearful foreboding, and I appealed to Mr. Barry, the 2d officer, for his opinion as to what would be Mr. Knight's probable course, remarking "He certainly will not disobey his orders." Mr. Barry, however, expressed his fears as to the result, remarking be knew so well the contempt which Mr. Knight entertained for these people, "that be will probably conclude your precautions to be altogether unnecessary, and that he can allow them to come on board with impunity, without your ever knowing anything of the circumstance, and no harm will come of it." This view of the case certainly did not have the effect, in any degree, to allay my anxiety, and I observed, "if your predictions prove correct, the ship is taken;" but concluding it to be altogether too' late for us on shore to render any assistance to the ship, and still clinging to the hope that Mr. Knight would, after all, be faithful to his trust, Mr. Barry and two men were directed to walk up towards the beach without any apparent concern, and watch the movements on board. I should have remarked, on my own way up to the beach, just before, I passed near a tree, under the shade of which a group of ten or twelve natives were apparently holding a consultation, and, as I approached, all conversation ceased. The object of this meeting, as I was afterwards informed, was to consider whether it would be better to kill us before attempting to take the ship, or afterward; and the conclusion arrived at was to be sure of the ship first, the killing of us appearing to them as easy, to use their own simile, as cutting off the heads of so many fowls : the manner how had already been decided, the time when was all there was to be considered,—a native having been already appointed, and the price fixed for the assassination of each of the boat's crew. The price set upon my life was 1000 dollars, for the 2d officer's, 500 dollars, and for each of the seamen 100 dollars. It was the business of my officious friend, whom I met that morning on landing, to bestow that delicate little piece of attention upon me.

As soon as Mr. Barry had reached an elevation where he could fairly see the ship's hull, I noticed a quick convulsive movement of his limbs, and that he turned short round, and walked, without hastening his steps, directly towards me;—passing me, however, without discovering any emotion, our eyes not being even directed towards each other, and said, "there is trouble on board. Sir,"— to the question "What did you see?" he replied, "Men jumping overboard." Convinced at once, of our own perilous situation, and that our escape depended on extremely cautious and judicious management, I answered "We must show no alarm, but muster the men, and order them immediately into the boat " At this moment we did not know, of course, whether it was the natives or our own crew who were jumping overboard, there was nothing certain further than that the ship was undoubtedly attacked, and we on shore must look out for our lives.— The men got into the boat in their usual deliberate manner, and winded her head round towards the mouth of the river, when Philip Manning, one of the crew, who had yet no suspicion of what was going on, reminded me I had not locked the chest containing the weights. And here I ought, perhaps, to remark that in this trade the weights are as much a matter of contract and bargain as the price of pepper, and for the bettor satisfaction of both parties I had recently adopted the plan of locking up the weights over-night in a chest kept on shore for that purpose. This was in the first place to prevent the Malays taking out the lead, and in the next, convincing them that we did not violate our part of the contract by putting any secretly in. Such is the mutual want of confidence manifested in our dealings with each other on this coast.

Everything being now in readiness, we pushed off from the shore, the Malays having no suspicion of our design, believing we intended to remain for the other boat load of pepper, and thinking it to be our intention, by our apparently unconcerned manner, to cross the river for a stroll in the opposite Bazar, as was our frequent custom. The moment the boat's stern had left the bank of the river, Po Adam sprang into her in a great state of excitement, to whom I exclaimed, "What! do you come too, Adam?"— he answered "You got trouble, captain, if they kill you, must kill Po Adam first." He suggested we should immediately steer the boat as far as possible from the western bank of the river, which was here not more than one hundred feet wide, when I remarked to the boat's crew, "now spring to your oars my lads for your lives, or we are all dead men." Adam exhibited the utmost alarm and consternation, encouraging my men to exert themselves, and talking English and Acheenise both in the same breath,— now exclaiming in Acheenise, *"di-yoong di yoong hi!"* and then exhorting them to *"pull, pull trong!"* The men worked with a will at their oars, and what with their efforts and the assistance of a favorable current, we made rapid progress out of the river. As we doubled one of the points we saw hundreds of natives rushing with wild impetuosity towards the river's mouth, brandishing their weapons, and otherwise menacing us.—Adam upon seeing this was struck with dismay, and exclaimed "'if got blunderbuss will kill all,"—but luckily they were not provided with that weapon, and we therefore escaped its dangers. A ferry-boat was next discovered with ten or twelve Malays in her, armed with long spears, evidently waiting to intercept us. I ordered Mr. Barry into the bows of the boat, and with Adam's sword to make demonstrations of being armed, and also to cun the boat in such a manner as to run down the ferry boat, which I concluded was our only chance to escape. Our own boat being a pinnace of some twenty-five feet in length, high out of water, and the ferry boat a long low canoe, the thing appeared quite feasible. With headlong impetuosity we were rushing towards our antagonist, nerved with the feeling of desperation. The distance between us was rapidly diminishing. With profound stillness and breathless anxiety we awaited the moment of collision, like a fated boat over the cataract of Niagara, with scarcely one chance in a thousand to escape death. The points of their pikes could be plainly seen. Already I observed

Mr. Barry with his sword elevated, as if in the act of striking. But when we had approached within some twenty feet, her crew all at once, as if by the direct interposition of Providence, appeared completely panic struck, and made an effort to get out of our way. It was, however, a close shave,—so close that one of their spears was actually over the stern of our boat, which with my hand, as we passed, I pushed aside. It was long before the countenances of those men, as they sat resting on their spears, faded from my recollection, so indelibly were they engraved on my memory. They often visited me in my dreams, and disturbed even my waking hours. We are not at all inclined to a belief in special providences, but this incident to my mind is as remarkable as the cessation of surf, related by Riley, which enabled him to escape from the shore out of the hands of the Arabs on the West Coast of Africa.—The Malays on the last point of the river as we passed, appeared perfectly frantic at our escape, and ran into the water up to their armpits, in their endeavors to intercept us, waving their swords above their heads, and shouting at the tops of their voices. Having now run the gauntlet, all danger for the present was passed, and during the breathing spell which it allowed us, we quietly proceeded the remainder of the distance out of the river without any further incident or molestation. We had now time calmly to contemplate the scene through which we had just passed, with hearts, I trust, grateful to God for his kind protection and safe guidance in the midst of its perils.— This was the part of their plan, otherwise well-conceived, which was defective,—they had taken no measures to prevent our escape from the shore, not believing for a moment that our lives were not at their disposal, unprotected and defenseless as they saw us.

The whole scene would furnish an admirable subject for the pencil of the artist,— the fragile boat running the gauntlet, and forcing her way through the narrow passage out of the river—notwithstanding the efforts of hundreds of Malays who are endeavoring to intercept her; the neighboring bazar and the points of the river crowded with natives, many of whom are actually in the water up to their arm-pits, while others are running to and fro, and all in a state of the greatest excitement, vociferating to the extent of their voices. The doomed ship laying tranquilly in the roads, with sails furled, and a pepper boat alongside, with a multitude of natives in every part of her, and none of her own crew visible, with the exception of a man on the top gallant yard and some ten of twelve heads just even with the surface of the water. High mountains in the back ground densely clothed with wood, and a long range of low thatched houses, with here and there a few cocoanut trees surrounding them, and a sandy beach of miles in extent, on which the surf is beating most furiously. Its well-drawn sketch could not fail to gratify the lovers of marvelous and thrilling adventures.

Having thus cleared the river, which was like passing the limits of the valley of the shadow of death, our first attention was directed to the ship, and judge of our feelings when, after a moment's observation, we were convinced she was captured. None of our crew, except one man aloft on the fore top gallant yard, could anywhere be seen, and the pirates were conspicuous in every part of her waving their cloths, and making evident signals ot success to the natives on shore. Without consideration my first impulse was to propose boarding her, and was very properly reminded that if the ship with her full armament had been taken with 80 many of her crew on board, we could do comparatively nothing in out unarmed state, towards her recapture; and the idea was as soon abandoned, as entertained,— if, indeed, it was ever seriously entertained at all.

We however continued to row up towards the ship until we could see the Malays pointing her muskets at us from the quarter deck, and that they appeared also to be clearing away the stem chasers, which we knew to be loaded to their muzzles with grape and langrage, which would be exceedingly unwelcome visitors in our defenseless situation to encounter. At this moment, three large Malay boats crowded with men, were seen coming out of the river, and to pull directly towards up. While debating what to do, and whether it would not be best to proceed at once to Muckie for assistance, which was some 25 miles distant, where we knew two or three American vessels were laying, heavy clouds commenced rolling down over the mountains, and the rumbling of distant thunder, and sharp flashes of lightning, gave sure indications that the land wind would be accompanied with deluges of rain, rendering the night, at least the first part ot it, one of Egyptian darkness, in which it would be almost impossible to grope our way safely along shore towards that place. Under those discouraging prospects, Po Adam advised us to proceed to Pulo Kio, and take shelter in his fort. Submitting ourselves almost wholly to his guidance, we at once pulled away for that place, but before we reached it his heart failed him, and he represented his fort as not sufficiently strong to resist a vigorous assault, if one should be made, and would not therefore be responsible for our lives, — but suggested we should proceed to Soosoo, which being some two miles further remote from the scene of the late outrage, he concluded we might be safe. We accordingly proceeded for Soosoo River, which we had scarcely entered when Po Adam's confidence again forsook him, and he advised us not to land. We therefore only filled a keg with water from the river and came out over the bar, intending to make the best of our way to Muckie, having more confidence, afterall, in the elements, than in the treacherous specimens of humanity with which we were then surrounded.

The night now came on dark and lowering, and just as we had left Soosoo river, the land wind, which had been some time retarded by a strong sea breeze, accompanied with heavy thunder and torrents of rain, overtook us, and came pelting down upon our unprotected heads. Sharp flashes of lightning occasionally shot across the gloom, which rendered the scene still more fearful. We double manned two of the oars with Mr. Barry and Po Adam, and I did the best I could to keep the boat's head down the coast, it being impossible to see any object on shore, or even to hear the surf, by which we could judge our distance from it. Having proceeded in this way until we begin to think ourselves near North Tallapow which was a dangerous shoal, it became a matter of concern how we should keep clear of it. We frequently laid upon our oars and listened, to ascertain if we could bear it break, but the noise of the elements rendered it impossible. Directly we felt the boat lifted upon a high wave, which we knew immediately must be the roller upon this shoal, which passing, broke with a fearful crash some three or four hundred feet from us. It is almost unnecessary to say, had we been that distance nearer the shore, it would have been the last known of *the Friendship*'s boat's crew, as the boat would undoubtedly have been dashed to pieces on the shoal, and all on board her must have perished. But through the kind protection of an all-merciful God, we were preserved from such a fate.

Having thus providentially passed this dangerous spot in safety, the weather began to clear a little, and here and there a star made its appearance, and looked compassionately down upon us. The off shore wind, too, became more steady and the rain ceased. To clear the boat ot the quantity of water which had rained into her, now occupied our first attention, which, however, we found a slow and tedious process, as we bad nothing larger than a tin pot to bail with. We also commenced ripping up some gunny bags which were left in the boat, and tying them together for a sail, under which we found the boat bounded along quite briskly; we therefore laid in our ours, all hands being now quite exhausted, and proceeded in this way the rest of the distance to Muckie, where we arrived at about one o'clock, A. M. We found here the ship *James Monroe,* Porter, of New York, brig *Gov. Endicott,* Jenks, of Salem, and brig *Palmer,* Powers, of Boston. On approaching the roads, we were first bailed from *the Gov. Endicott,* and to the question "What boat is that?" the response was, "the *Friendship*'s, from Quallah Batoo," which answer was immediately followed with the question "Is that you, Capt. Endicott?" "Yes," was the answer, "with all that are left of us." It was but the work of a moment to clamber up her sides on to her decks, where we were instantly surrounded with captain, officers and crew, all anxious to learn the particulars of our sad misfortune. We could tell them only of our own adventures; the circumstances of the capture of the ship, and the massacre of part of her crew, were to be hereafter revealed.

Having communicated with the other vessels, their commanders repaired on board *the Gov. Endicott*, when it was instantly concluded to proceed with their vessels to Quallah Batoo, and endeavor to recover the ship. These vessels were laying with most of their sails unbent, but their decks were quickly all life and animation, and the work of bending sails proceeded so rapidly that before three o'clock all the vessels were out of the roads and beading up the coast towards Quallah Batoo. Both the land and sea breeze were light throughout the day, and it was not until about the middle of the afternoon that we sighted the ship. Every arrangement was now made for her capture. It was our intention to throw as many of the crews of *the Gov. Endicott* and *Palmer* as could be prudently spared, on board *the James Monroe*, being the largest vessel, and proceed with her directly into the roads, and lay her alongside *the Friendship*, and carry her by boarding,—the other vessels following at a short distance. But as soon as we had completed all our arrangements, and while we were yet several miles outside the port, the sea breeze began to fail us, with indications that the land wind, like that of the day before, would be accompanied with heavy rain. We however stood on towards the place until the off shore wind and rain reached us, when all three vessels were obliged to anchor, and suspend further operations until the next morning. Before dark I had taken the bearings of the ship by compass, intending, if circumstances favored it, to propose a descent upon her during the night; but the heavy rain continued the most part of it, and we were baffled in that design. The first indications of daylight found us upon the decks of *the Monroe*, watching for the ship, which, in the yet indistinct light, could not be discerned in the roads. The horizon in the offing was also searched unsuccessfully with our glasses; but as objects became more distinct we at last discovered her close in shore, far to the westward of her late anchorage, inside a large cluster of dangerous shoals, to which position, as it then appeared, the Malays must have removed her during the night. What I now most apprehended was that they bad got her upon one of the reefs, and if so, her recapture would have been useless; but when the day had sufficiently advanced to enable us with our glasses to make a careful examination of her position, to our great relief we ascertained this was not the case. One thing was however, certain, we could not carry out our original design of running her alongside in her present situation; the navigation would be too dangerous for either of the ships, and must therefore be abandoned. At this moment we saw a Prou, or Malay trading craft, approaching the roads from the westward, with which I communicated, and of which I hired a canoe, and sent a messenger on shore to inform the Rajahs if they would give the ship up peaceably to us we would not molest them, otherwise we should fire both upon her and the town. This was considered the most advisable course; all the fleet being in pursuit of cargoes, some apprehensions began to be entertained lest hostilities should be the means of breaking up their voyages, or at least vitiating their insurance. After waiting considerable time for the return of the messenger, during which we could see boats passing close in shore from the ship loaded with plunder, we concluded this delay was only a subterfuge to gain farther time for that purpose, and we fired a gun across the bows of one of them, which arrested her progress. In a few minutes the canoe which we had sent on shore was seen putting off. The answer received, however, was one of defiance, — "that they should not give her up so easily, but we might take her if we could." All three vessels then opened their fires upon the town and ship, which was returned by the forts on shore, the Malays also firing our ship's guns at us. The first shot from one of the forts passed between the masts of the *Gov. Endicott*, not ten feet above the heads of the crew, and the second struck the water just under her counter. This vessel had been kedged in close to the shore within point blank shot of the fort, with springs upon her cable, determined on making every gun tell. The spirited manner in which their fire was returned soon silenced this fort, which mounted six six-pounders and several small brass pieces. It appeared afterward, by the testimony of one of the crew, who was confined here, that the firing was so effectual that it dismounted their guns and split the carriages. The other two forts, which were situated at a greater distance from the beach, continued firing, and no progress was made towards re-capturing the ship, which, after all, was our only object. It was now between three and four o'clock; and the land wind began to make demonstrations of another rainy night, and it was certain if the Malays were allowed to hold possession on of the ship much longer, they would either get her on shore, or burn her. We then held a council of war on board *the Monroe,* and concluded to board her with as large a force as we could carry in three boats; and that the command of the expedition should of course devolve upon me. Just at this juncture the ship ceased firing, and we observed a column of smoke rise from her decks abreast the mainmast, and that there appeared to be great confusion on board. We subsequently ascertained that they blew themselves up by setting fire to an open keg of powder, from which they were loading the guns, after having expended all the cartridges. Everything being in readiness for our expedition, we pushed off. The ship lay with her port side towards us, and, with the intention of getting out of the range of her guns, pulled to the westward at an angle of some 33 deg., until we opened her starboard bow, when we bore up in three divisions for boarding, one at each gangway, and the other over the bows. We were now before the wind, and two oars in each boat were sufficient to propel them; the rest of the crew, armed to the teeth with markets, cutlasses and pistols, sat quietly in their places, their muskets pointed at the ship, as the boats approached. The Malays for the first time seemed to contemplate our design, and as we neared the ship were struck with consternation and commenced deserting her with all possible dispatch and in the greatest confusion. The numerous boats of all description alongside were immediately filled, and those who could find no other means of conveyance, jumped overboard and swam for the shore. The beach was consequently lined with boats, and the Malays took to the jungle with the greatest precipitation, so that when we reach the ship, there was, to all appearance, no one on board. Still fearing some treachery, we approached with the same caution and boarded her, cutlass in hand, in the same order we should have done had we known her to be full of men. Having reached her decks and finding them deserted, before we laid aside our arms, a strict search was instituted throughout the ship, with instructions to cut down any who should be found, and give no quarter. But she was completely forsaken, not a soul on board. Her appearance at the time we boarded her defies description, suffice it to say that every part of her bore ample testimony to the scene of violence and destruction with which she had been visited. That many lives had been sacrificed, her blood-stained decks abundantly testified. We found her within pistol-shot of the beach, with most of her sails cut loose, and flying from the yards. Why they had not succeeded in their attempts to get her on shore, was soon apparent. A riding turn in the chain around the windlass, which they were not sailors enough to clear, had no doubt prevented it. There had been evidently a fruitless attempt to cut it off. While we were clearing the chain, and preparing to kedge the ship off into the roads, the Malays, still bent upon annoying us, and unwilling to abandon their prize, were seen drawing a gun over the sandy beach upon a drag, directly under our stern, which, having fired, it jumped off the carriage and was abandoned. The rain, with the land their places, with their muskets pointed at the wind, now set in again; it was, however, the ship as the boats approached. The Malays now, for the first time, seemed to comprehend our design, and as we neared the ship, were struck with consternation, and commenced deserting her with all possible dispatch, and in the greatest confusion. The numerous boats of all descriptions, alongside, were immediately filled, and those who could find no work of but a short lime to kedge the ship off into deep water, and anchor her in comparative security alongside the other ships in the roads.

The next morning a canoe was seen approaching *the James Monroe*, from Pulo Kio, with five or six men in her, whom we took, as a matter of course, to be natives; but we were other means of conveyance, jumped overboard soon hailed from that ship, and informed that and swam for the shore. The beach was consequently lined with boats, and the Malays took to the jungle with the greatest precipitation, so that when we reached the ship, there was, to all appearance, no one on board. Still fearing some treachery, we other with the same caution, and boarded her, cutlass in hand, in the same order we should have done had we known her to be full of men.— Having reached her decks, and finding them four of the number were a part of our own crew, I proceeded immediately on board and found them to be Wm. Parnell, John Muzzey, Algernon Warren, seamen, and Wm. Bray, carpenter. Their haggard and squalid appearance bespoke what they had suffered. It would seem impossible that in the space of four days, men could, by any casualty, so entirely lose their identity. They bore no semblance to their former selves, and it was only deserted, before we laid aside our arms a strict by asking their names that I knew either of search was instituted throughout the ship, them. They were without clothing, other than loose pieces of cotton cloth thrown over their persons, their hair matted, their bodies crisped and burnt in large running blisters, besides having nearly been devoured by mosquitos, the poison of whose stings had left evidence of its virulence; their flesh wasted away, even the tones of their voices were changed. It is no exaggeration to say their appearance forcibly reminded me of the print of Capt. Riley and his men at their first interview of Mr. Willshire[1] under the palace walls at Mogadore. The few pieces of cloth, which cov-

---

[1] *Shipwrecked, and enslaved in 1815 Morocco, Riley's crew were in a terrible state when ransomed and recovered by Vice Counsel Willshire.*

ered their nakedness, being all they could bear, and these it was necessary to oil, to enable them to do even that. They had been wandering about in the jungle without food since the ship was taken, and the story of their sufferings was a painful one. The account of the capture of the ship was as follows: — When the pepperboat came alongside, it was observed by the crew that all on board her were strangers, and not one was recognized as having been off to the ship before. They were also better dressed than boatmen generally, all of them having on white or yellow jackets, and new ivory-handled krises. No notice appeared to be taken of these suspicious circumstances by the mate, and all except two men, who were left to pass up pepper, were admitted indiscriminately to come on board. One of the crew, named Wm. Parnell, who was stationed at the gangway to pass along pepper, made some remark, to call his attention to the number of natives on board, and was answered in a gruffy manner, and asked if he was afraid. No, replied the man, not afraid; but I know it to be contrary to the regulations of the ship. He was ordered, with an oath, to pass along pepper, and mind his own business. The natives were also seen by the crew sharpening their krises upon the grindstone, which stood upon the forecastle, and a man named Chester, who was subsequently killed while starting pepper down the forehatch, asked them in pantomime, for he could not speak the language, what so many of them wanted on board, and was answered in the same way, that they came off to see the ship. He was heard by one of the crew to say, "we must look out you do not come for anything worse," at the same time drawing a handspike within his reach. The Malays had distributed themselves about the decks in the most advantageous manner for an attack, and at some pre-concerted signal a simultaneous assault upon the crew was made in every part of the ship. Two Malaya were seen by the steward to rush with their krises upon Mr. Knight, who was very badly stabbed in the back and side, the weapons appearing to be buried in his body, up to their very hilts.— Chester, at the fore hatch, notwithstanding his distrust and precaution, was killed outright, and supposed to have fallen into the hold. The steward, at the galley, was also badly wounded, and was only saved from death by the kris striking hard against a short rib, which took the force of the blow. Of the two men on the stage over the ship's side, one was killed, and the other so badly wounded as to be made a cripple for life. The chief officer was seen, after he was stabbed, to rush aft upon the starboard side of the quarter deck, and endeavor to get a boarding pike out of the beckets, abreast the mizzen rigging, where he was met by Parnell, to whom be exclaimed, "do your duty," at the same instant two or three Malays rushed upon him, and he was afterwards seen lying dead near the same spot, with the boarding pike under him. On the instant the crew found the ship attacked they attempted to get aft into the cabin for arms, but the Malaya had placed a guard on each side of the companion-way, which prevented them; they then rushed forward for handspikes, and were again intercepted; and being completely bewildered, surprised and defenseless, and knowing that several of their shipmates had already been killed outright before their eyes, and others wounded, all who could swim plunged overboard, and the others took to the rigging, or crept over the bows out of sight. The decks were now cleared, and the pirates had full possession of the ship. The men in the water then consulted together what they should do, concluding it certain death to return to the ship; and they determined it would be the safest to swim on shore, and secrete themselves in the jungle;—but as they approached it they observed the beach about Quallah Batoo lined with natives, and they proceeded more to the westward, and landed upon a point called Ouj'ong Lamah Moodah, nearly two miles distant from the ship. On their way they bad divested themselves of every article of clothing, and they were entirely naked at the time they landed. As it was not yet dark, they sought safety and seclusion in the jungle, from whence they emerged as soon as they thought it safe, and walked upon the beach in the direction of Cape Felix and Annalaboo, intending to make the best of their way to the latter place, with the hope of meeting there some American vessel, on board which they would find shelter and protection. At the approach of daylight they sought a hiding-place again in the bushes; but it afforded them only a partial protection from the scorching rays of the sun, from which, being entirely naked, they experienced the most dreadful effects. Hunger and thirst began also to make demands upon them; but no food could anywhere be found. They tried to eat grass, but their stomachs refused it. They found a few husks of the cocoanut, which they chewed, endeavoring to extract some nourishment from them, but in vain. They stayed in their hiding-place the whole of this day, and saw Malays passing along the beach, but were afraid to discover themselves. At night they pursued their journey again, during which they passed several small streams, where they slaked their thirst, but obtained no food. About midnight they came to a very broad river, which they did not venture to cross. The current was very rapid, and they had no means of conveyance other than their own limbs, and having been 36 hours without food of any kind, they did not dare attempt it. This river I have always supposed to be Quallah Toepah, about midway between Cape Felix and Annalaboo. Here, then, they were put completely hors de combat; they found for want of food their energies were fast giving way, and still they believed their lives depended on not being discovered. I have since been struck with the Remarks of Dr. Kane, on the effects of a want of food, which are so much like the account given by my men, that I cannot refrain from, inserting it. "The first symptom," says he, does not show itself in hunger, but in a loss of power often so imperceptibly brought on that it becomes evident only by an accident— such, for instance, as the inability felt to cross this river. Since further progress towards Annalaboo appeared impossible, they resolved to retrace their steps, endeavor to pass Quallah Batoo in the night, without being discovered, and reach the hospitable residence of Po Adam, at Pulo Kio. They accordingly took up their line of march towards that place, immediately, and reached, as they supposed, the neighborhood of Cape Felix by the morning, when they again retreated to the jungle, where they lay concealed another day, being Wednesday, the day of the recapture of the ship, but at too great distance to hear the firing. At night they again resumed their journey, and having reached the spot where the Malays landed in so much haste when they deserted the ship, they found the beach covered with canoes, a circumstance which aroused their suspicions, but for which they were at a loss to account. They now concluded each to take a canoe, as the most certain way of passing Quallah Batoo without discovery, and so proceed to Pulo Kio. As they passed the roads, they heard one of the ship's bells strike the hour, and the well-known cry of "All's well," but fearing it was some decoy of the natives, they would not approach her, but proceeded on their way, and landed at Pulo Kio, secreting themselves once more in the jungle, neap the residence of Po Adam, until the morning, when four naked and half-famished white men were seen to emerge from the bushes, and approach his fort with feeble steps, who, as soon as recognized, were welcomed by him with the strongest demonstrations of delight; slapping his bands, shouting at the top of his lungs, and in the exuberance of his joy committing all kinds of extravagances. They now heard of the recapture of the ship, and the escape of the boat's crew on shore, which it had never occurred to them were not already numbered with the dead. They were clothed as we have described, and a breakfast of boiled rice prepared, being the first food that they had tasted for the period of 72 hours. Having refreshed themselves, they were conveyed by Adam and his men on board *the James Munroe*, in the pitiful condition of which we have before spoken.

In the course of the latter part of the same day, another canoe, with a white flag displayed, was observed approaching the fleet from the direction of Quallah Batoo, containing three or four Chinamen, who informed us that four of our men, two of whom were wounded, one very severely, were at their houses on shore, where their wounds had been dressed, and they had been otherwise cared for; and that we could ransom them of the Rajahs at ten dollars each. To this I readily agreed, and they were soon brought off to the ship in a sampan, and proved to be Charles Converse and Gregorie Pedechio, seamen, Lorenzo Migell, cook, and William Francis, steward. Converse was laid out at full length upon a board, as if dead,—evidently very badly wounded. The story of the poor fellow was a sad one, lie, with John Davis, being the two tallest men in the ship, were on the stage over the side when she was attacked. Their first impulse was, to gain the ship's decks, but were defeated in this design by the pirates, who stood guard over the gangway, and making repeated thrusts at them. They then made a desperate attempt to pass over the pepper-boat, and thus gain the water, in doing which they were both most severely wounded. Having reached the water, Converse swam round to the ship's bows, and grasped the chain, to which he clang as well as be was able, being badly crippled in one of his hands, with other severe wounds in various parts of his body. When it became dark, he crawled up over the bows as well as his exhausted strength from the loss of blood would permit, and crept to the foot of the forecastle stairs, where he supposed he must have fainted, and fell prostrate upon the floor without the power of moving himself one inch further. The Malays believing him dead, took no heed of him, but travelled up and down over his body the whole night. Upon attempting to pass over the boat, after being foiled in his endeavor to reach the ship's decks, a native made a pass at his head with his "parrung," a weapon resembling most a butcher's cleaver, which he warded off by throwing up his naked arm, and the force of the blow fell upon the outer part of his hand, severing all the bones and sinews belonging to three of his fingers, and leaving untouched only the fore finger and thumb. Besides this he received a kris wound in the back, which must have penetrated to the stomach, from whence he bled from his mouth the most part of the night. He was likewise very badly wounded in the ham just below the groin, which came so nearly through the leg as to discolor the flesh upon the inside. Wonderful, however, to relate, notwithstanding the want of proper medical advice, and with nothing but the unskillful treatment of three or four ship masters, the thermometer ranging all the time, from 85 to 90 deg., this man recovered from his wounds, but in his crippled hand, he carried the marks of Malay perfidy to his watery grave, having been drowned at sea from on board of the brig *Fair American*, in the winter of 1833-4, which was, no doubt, occasioned by this wound, which unfitted him for holding on properly while aloft.

The fate of his companion Davis, was a tragic one. He could not swim, and after I reaching the water was seen to struggle hard to gain the boat's tackle full at the stern, to which he clung until the Malays dropped the pepper boat astern, when he was observed apparently imploring mercy at their hands, which the wretches did not heed, but butchered him upon the spot. Gregory was the man seen aloft when we had cleared the river, cutting strange antics which we did not at the time comprehend. By his account, when he reached the fore topgallant yard, the pirates commenced firing the ship's muskets at him, which he dodged by getting over the front side of the yard and sail and down upon the collar of the stay, and then reversing the movement. John Masury related that after being wounded in the side, he crept over the bow of the ship and down upon an anchor, where he was sometime employed in dodging the thrusts of a boarding pike in the hands of a Malay, until the arrival of a reinforcement from the shore, when every-one fearing lest he should not get his full share of plunder, ceased further to molest the wounded. The story of the steward has already been told.

The ship, the first night after her capture, according to the testimony of these men, was a perfect pandemonium, and a Babel of the most discordant sounds. The ceaseless moaning of the surf upon the adjacent shore, the heavy peals of thunder, and sharp flashings of lightning directly over their heads,—the sighing of the wind in wild discords through the rigging, like the wailings of woe from the manes of their murdered shipmates; and all this intermingled with the more earthly sounds of the squealing of pigs, the screeching of fowls, the cackling of roosters, the unintelligible jargon of the natives, jangling and vociferating, with horrible laughter, shouts and yells, in every part of her, and in the boats alongside carrying off plunder; their black figures unexpectedly darting forth from every unseen quarter, as if rising up and again disappearing through the decks, and gamboling about in the dark, so like a saturnalia of demons, that it was easy to fancy the fumes of sulfur were actually invading their olfactories, and the whole scene more fully realized their ideas of the infernal regions, than anything with which their imaginations could compare it. It is the general impression that Malays, being Mussulmen[1], have a holy horror of swine, as unclean animals; the very touch of which imposes many ablutions, and abstaining from food for several days together,—but, according to the testimony of my men, it was perfectly marvelous how they handled, that night, those on board our ship,—going into their pens, seizing, struggling, and actually *embracing* them, until they succeeded in throwing every one overboard.

The morning succeeding her capture, affairs on board appeared to be getting to be a little more settled, when several Chinamen came off and performed the part of good Samaritans, in taking the wounded men on shore to their houses, and dressing their wounds with some simple remedies, which at least kept down inflammation. In doing this, however, they were obliged to barricade their dwellings, to guard them against the insulting annoyances of the natives.

Quallah Batoo bazar that day presented a ludicrous spectacle. Almost every Malay was decked out in a white, blue, red, checked, or striped shirt, or some other European article of dress or manufacture, stolen from the ship, not even excepting the woolen table cloth belonging to the cabin, which was seen displayed over the shoulders of a native,—all seemingly quite proud of their appearance, and strutting about with a solemn

---

[1] *mussulmen:* "Muslim"

gravity and oriental self-complacency, that was perfectly ludicrous. Their novel and grotesque appearance could not fail to suggest the idea that a tribe of monkeys had made a descent upon some unfortunate clothing establishment, and each to have seized and carried off whatever article of dress was most suited to his taste and fancy.

According to Gregory, who, not being wounded, remained on board, the ship was all day filled with Malays searching into every possible nook and cranny where they thought money might be secreted, and carrying off the very trifles which could be of no use to them. In the afternoon, on the appearance of the fleet from Muckie, they were determined on running her ashore, lest she should be re-taken, and with that view commenced weighing anchor, and everything for some time gave assurances of the fulfilment of their wishes.—The ship was already drifting towards the beach, when the anchor came in sight, and they let go the chain, ceased heaving at the windlass, and made a rush forward to see it. At this moment the weight of the anchor caused the chain to commence running out with great velocity, and when some 12 or 13 fathoms had thus disappeared, it jumped, and caught a riding turn around the windlass, which brought it to a stand. Poor Gregory was now brought forward to clear it,— but he persisted it was past his skill, which of course they did not believe, and tied him in the rigging, and made demonstrations of ripping him open, flourishing their knives in fearful proximity about his person in a state of great exasperation. They next made a fruitless attempt to cut it off with the cook's axe. Thus matters stood, when the land wind with heavy rain set in, and the natives sought shelter in the cabin, leaving the ship to her fate and she drifted to the westward into shoal water, where the anchor again took hold and brought her up in the place we discovered her the next morning, and where we boarded and took possession of her. Gregory was then taken on shore, and confined in the fort, which was silenced by *the Gov. Endicott.*

The ship was now once more in our possession, with what of her cargo and crew. She was rifled of almost every movable article on board, and scarcely anything but her pepper remaining. Of our outward cargo every dollar of spice, and every pound of opium had of course become a prey to them. All her spare sails and rigging were gone—not a needle or ball of twine, palm, marling spike, or piece of rope were left! All our charts, chronometers and other nautical instruments—all our clothing and bedding, were also gone; as well as our cabin furniture and small stores of every description. Our ship's provisions, such as beef, pork and most of our bread, had, however, been spared. Of our armament nothing but the large guns remained. Every pistol, musket, cutlass, and boarding pike, with our entire stock of powder, had been taken.

With assistance from the other vessels we immediately began making the necessary preparations to leave the port with all possible dispatch, but owing to much rainy weather we did not accomplish it for three days after recapturing the ship, when we finally succeeded in leaving the place in company with the fleet bound for South Tallapow, where we arrived on the 14th February. When we landed at this place with the other masters and super cargoes, we were followed through the streets of the bazar by the natives in great crowds, exulting and hooting, with exclamations similar to these, — "Who great man now, Malay or American?" "How many man American dead?" "How many man Malay dead?"

We now commenced in good earnest to prepare our ship for sea. Our voyage had been broken up, and there was nothing left for us but to return to the United States. We finally left Muckie, whither we had already proceeded, on the 27th February, for Pulo Kio, accompanied by ship *Delphos*, Capt. James D. Gillie, and *the Gov. Endicott*, Capt. Jenks, where I was yet in hopes to recover some of my nautical instruments. With the assistance of Po Adam, I succeeded in obtaining, for a moderate sum, my sextant and one of my chronometers, which enabled me to navigate the ship. We sailed from Pulo Kio on the

4th of March, and arrived at Salem on the 16th of July. The intense interest and excitement caused by our arrival may still be remembered. It being nearly calm, as we approached the harbor, we were boarded several miles outside by crowds of people, all anxious to learn the most minute particulars of our sad misfortune, the news of which had preceded us by the arrival of a China ship at New York, which we had met at St. Helena. The curiosity of some of our visitors was so great that they would not be satisfied until they knew the exact spot where every man stood, who was either killed or wounded. Even the casing of the cabin, so much cut up in search of money, or other valuables, was an object of the greatest interest.

But the feeling of presumptuous exultation and proud defiance exhibited by the natives, was of brief duration. The avenger was at hand. In something less than a year after this outrage, the U. S. Frigate *Potomac*, Com. Downes, appeared off the port of Quallah Batoo, and anchored in the outer roads, disguised as a merchantman. Every boat which visited her from the shore was detained, that her character might not be made known to the natives. Several amusing anecdotes were told, of the fear and terror exhibited in the countenances of the natives, when they so unexpectedly found themselves imprisoned within the wooden walls of the Potomac, surrounded by such a formidable armament, which bespoke the errand that had attracted her to their shores. They prostrated themselves at full length upon her decks, trembling in the most violent manner, and appearing to think nothing but certain death awaited them—which it required all the efforts of the officers to dispel.

A reconnoitering party was first sent on shore, professedly for the purpose of traffic.— But when they approached, the natives came down to the beach in such numbers, it excited their suspicions that her character and errand had somehow preceded her, and it was considered prudent not to land. Having, therefore, examined the situation of the forts and the means of defense, they returned to the frigate. The same night some 300 men, under the guidance of Mr. Barry, the former 2d officer of *the Friendship*, who was assistant sailing-master of the frigate, landed to the westward of the place, with the intention of surprising the forts and the town, but by some unaccountable delay, the morning was just breaking when the detachment had effected a landing, and as they were marching along the beach towards the nearest fort, a Malay came out of it, by whom they were discovered, and an alarm given. They however pushed on, and captured the forts by storm, after some hard fighting, and set fire to the town, which was burnt to ashes. The natives, not even excepting the women, fought with great desperation in the forts, many of whom would not yield until shot down or sabered on the spot. The next day the frigate was dropped in within gunshot, and bombarded the place, to impress them with the power and ability of the United States to avenge any act of piracy, or other indignity offered by them to her flag.—When I visited the coast again, some five months after this event, I found the department of the natives materially changed. There was now no longer exhibited either arrogance or proud defiance. All appeared impressed with the irresistible power of a nation that could send such tremendous engines of war as *the Potomac* frigate upon their shores, to avenge any wrongs committed upon its vessels; and that it would in future be better policy for them to attend to their pepper plantations, and cultivate the arts of peace, than subject themselves to such severe retribution as had followed this act of piracy upon *the Friendship*.

Perhaps, in justice to Po Adam, I ought to remark, before closing, that the account circulated by his countrymen of his conniving at, if not being actually connected with this piracy, a falsehood with which they found the means of deceiving several American Shipmasters, soon after the affair, is a base calumny against a worthy man, and has no foundation whatever in truth. The property he had in my possession on board the ship, in gold ornaments of various kinds, besides money, amounting to several thousand dollars, all of which he lost by the capture of the ship, and never recovered, bears ample testimony to the falsity of this charge. His countrymen also worked upon the avarice and cupidity of the king by misrepresentations of his exertions to recover the ship, thereby preventing them from making him a present of her, which they pretended was their intention. His sable majesty, in consequence, absolved every one of his debtors, all along the coast, from paying him their debts. He also confiscated all his property he could find, such as fishing-boats, nets and lines, and other fishing tackle, and appropriated the proceeds to his own use, so that ho was at once reduced to penury. All this wag in accordance with Commodore Bieulieu's account, already cited, upwards of two hundred years before, viz: "If they even suspect that any one bears them an ill will, they endeavor to ruin him by false accusations." The king also sent a small schooner down the coast, soon after, to reap further vengeance upon Po Adam. Arriving at Pulo Kio, while Adam was absent, the rifled his fort of everything valuable, and even took the ornaments, such as armlets and anklets, off the person of his wife. Intelligence having been conveyed to Po Adam of this outrage, he arrived home in the night before the schooner had left the harbor, and incensed, as it was natural he should be, at such base and cowardly treatment, he immediately opened a fire upon her and sunk her in nine feet of water. She was afterwards fished up by *the Potomac* frigate, and converted into fire-wood.

We do not know if Po Adam is now living, but some sixteen years since, we saw a letter from him to one of our eminent merchants, asking for assistance from our citizens, and stating truthfully all the facts in his case. I endeavored at the time, through our then representative to Congress, to bring the matter before that body, but from some cause it did not succeed, and the poor fellow has been allowed to live, if not to die, in his penury. We will, however, permit him to state his own case, in his own language, which he does in the following letter, written at his own dictation —

Quallah Batoo, 7th October, 1841.

To Joseph Peabody, Esq., of Salem, Mass

Some years have passed since the capture of *the Friendship*, commanded by my old friend, Capt. Endicott.

It perhaps is not known to you, that, by saving the life of Capt. Endicott, and the ship itself from destruction, it became, in consequence, a victim to the hatred and vengeance of my misguided countrymen; some time since, the last of my property was set on fire and destroyed, and now, for having been the steadfast friend of Americans, I am not only destitute, but an object of derision to my countrymen.

You, who are so wealthy and so prosperous, I have thought, that, if acquainted with these distressing circumstances, that you would not turn a deaf ear to my present condition.

I address myself to you, because through my agency many of your ships have obtained cargoes, but I respectfully beg that you will have the kindness to state my case to the rich pepper merchants of Salem and Boston, firmly believing that from their generosity, and your own, I shall not have reason to regret the warm and sincere friendship ever displayed toward your Captains, and all other Americans trading on this Coast.

I take the liberty, also, to subjoin a copy of a letter, recently received from Capt. Hammond, of the ship *Maria*, of New York; as he left this place lately, it will show whether I have been telling you otherwise than the melancholy truth, or grieve without a cause.

Wishing you. Sir, and your old companions in the Sumatra trade, and their Captains, health and prosperity, and trusting that, before many moons 1 shall, through your assistance, be released from my present wretched condition, believe me very respectfully,

Your faithful servant,
(signed) PO ADAM,
in Arabic characters.

Copy of the letter from Capt. Hammond above referred to

Soosoo, 21 July, 1841.

To the Commander of any U. S. Ship of War, touching on the West Coast of Sumatra:

This may certify that the bearer, Po Adam, at present residing at Quallah Batoo, has applied to me to write this statement of his situation, that he can present it as above.

I therefore state the following: I have been acquainted with him for the last twenty-five years, and have known him in prosperity and in adversity the same. It is well known that he was the principal means of saving the life of Capt. Charles M. Endicott, with his boat's crew, at the time that they captured *the Friendship*, of Salem, and by that act he has lost his property, and incurred the hatred and jealousy of the Acheenise. He is the most intelligent man among them, and one of the best pilots; is ever ready to render assistance to any American, and as he is at present very destitute, it would be an act of charity, as well as duty, if the American Government would assist him in his present circumstances.

He wishes to proceed to the United States to visit his old friends, and wishes to go in some Ship of War, of our nation. I hope his request may be granted, as he would there find influential men to represent his case to the Government of the United States.

(signed,) John Hammond
Master of the ship *Maria*, of New York,
and a resident of Salem.

GENERAL INSTRUCTIONS TO COMMODORE JOHN DOWNES, OF THE FRIGATE POTOMAC, AND INSTRUCTIONS TO SEEK REDRESS FOR THE DESTRUCTION OF THE SHIP FRIENDSHIP, AT QUALLAH BATOO, ISLAND OF SUMATRA, AND HIS REPORT RELATIVE TO THE DESTRUCTION OF THE TOWN OF QUALLAH BATOO.

COMMUNICATED TO THE HOUSE OF REPRESENTATIVES, JULY 13, 1832.

Washington City, July 12, 1832.

TO THE SPEAKER OF THE HOUSE OF REPRESENTATIVES:

Sir: In compliance with the resolution of the House of Representatives, passed this day, requesting the President of the United States "to lay before the House copies of the instructions given to the commander of the frigate Potomac, previous to and since the departure of that ship from the Island of Sumatra, and copies of such letters as may have been received from said commander after his arrival at Quallah Batoo, except such parts as may, in his judgment, require secrecy," I forward copies of the two letters of instructions to Captain Downes, in relation to the piratical plunder and murder of our citizens at Quallah Batoo, on the coast of Sumatra, detailing his proceedings.

The instructions, with the papers annexed, are all that have been given bearing on this subject; and, although parts of them do not relate materially to the supposed object of the resolution, yet it has been deemed expedient to omit nothing contained in the originals.

The letter and report from Captain Downes, which are herewith furnished, are all yet received from him, bearing upon his proceedings at Quallah Batoo; but as further intelligence may hereafter be communicated by him, I send the in for the information of the House; submitting, however, injustice to that officer, that their contents should not be published until he can enjoy a further opportunity of giving more full explanations of all the circumstances under which he conducted.

ANDREW JACKSON.

Navy Department, June 21, 1831.

TO COMMODORE JOHN DOWNES, OF THE FRIGATE POTOMAC:

Sir: When the frigate Potomac is in readiness to leave Norfolk, you will proceed to New York without delay, that her complete preparation and equipment may be effected at the navy yard there.

When she is in every respect ready for sea, which must certainly be accomplished by the first day of August next, you will receive on board the Hon. Martin Van Buren, minister from the United States to England, and his suite, and immediately make sail; shaping your course for Portsmouth, on the southern coast of England, or for any other port within the British Channel which you may find to be more safe and convenient, where you will land Mr. Van Buren and suite.

After fulfilling this part of your instructions, you will, with all practicable dispatch, direct your course for the Pacific Ocean, and assume the command of the naval forces of the United States on that station. You will touch on your way out at Porto Praya, of the Cape de Verde Islands, if not inconvenient, and also at Pernambuco, St. Salvador, and Rio de Janeiro, on the coast of Brazil, and communicate with the consuls or commercial agents of the United States at these ports, and render every lawful aid and protection to the persons and property of our citizens which may be needed; not, however, making any unnecessary delay at either of these places.

On your arrival in the Pacific, you will obtain from Master Commandant Gregory all necessary information relating to our commerce and squadron, and adopt suitable measures for executing and accomplishing the instructions and objects which he has not had it in his power to fulfill previous to your arrival.

A copy of his orders is furnished.

The force under your command will consist of the *Potomac*, as flag ship; the sloop-of-war *Falmouth*, Master Commandant Gregory; and the schooner *Dolphin*, Lieutenant John C. Long.

It is hoped that the force in the Pacific will be competent to afford sufficient protection to our extensive and important interests in that region of the world; and, placing every confidence in your skill, intelligence, and judgment, no doubt is entertained of your using every exertion in your power fully to accomplish the objects of your command.

You will on all occasions render, to our citizens, vessels, commerce, and interests, that assistance and protection to which they are lawfully entitled.

For your information and government in the execution of the duties assigned to you, I transmit a volume containing the treaties concluded between the United States and foreign powers, a compilation of the laws of the United States relating to the navy, a circular respecting the discharge of our seamen in foreign ports; another, directing a quarterly report to be made of American vessels boarded; and a third, regulating the official intercourse between the commanders of our ships-of-war and the consuls of the United States in foreign ports.

It is important that you should keep yourself always correctly advised of passing events; and it is, therefore, advisable that you commence and continue a regular correspondence with our public and commercial agents within the limits of your station.

Cases may arise which it is impossible to foresee, and to meet which definite instructions cannot be given; should such occur, out of the ordinary way, you must be left to the exercise of a sound discretion.

Our relations with the governments of the southern continent of America, as well as with Mexico, are on the most friendly footing; and care should be taken to abstain from any act which may impair their present character, so far as this can be done consistently with the maintenance of our own just rights.

You will be careful, on entering any harbor, or meeting a public vessel of another nation, to manifest the accustomed civilities; as we confidently expect them to be paid to us, it becomes us to be prompt in tendering them to others.

At all places you may visit, you will encourage the best feelings towards our government, nation, citizens, and interests; exhibiting, wherever an opportunity offers, that moderation and urbanity which become your own character and that of the government you represent.

Should war arise on the western coast of America, it will be recollected that the belligerent parties are entitled to equal rights; and the utmost caution must be observed to refrain from all acts towards either of them that might have a tendency to affect or compromise our neutral character. Acts of kindness to either, although equally extended to the others, might be misconceived or misconstrued to our prejudice. You will, therefore, to avoid all causes of complaint, decline, if requested, taking on board the vessels of your squadron, for either party, men, money, provisions, or supplies, to be carried for such party to any port or country whatever.

If hostilities should take place, it is probable that the parties will resort, as formerly, to the system of blockades, without an adequate force to maintain that mode of annoyance, and to the great injury and inconvenience of neutral vessels and commerce.

In the event of such a state of things, you will use your best efforts to protect our citizens and their property from the illegal exercise of power; claiming for them all the rights and privileges to which they are entitled by the laws of nations. At the same time you will avoid, as much as possible, all collision with either party, without compromitting, in any manner, our own just rights and national honor.

It is to be feared that some of the freebooters, whose depredations have been so successfully checked in the West Indies, and some of the privateers and parties employed during the wars which have existed in that quarter, may change the scene and character of their operations, in hopes of finding our commerce in a defenseless state. To guard against such an occurrence will require, on the part of the vessels under your command, the utmost vigilance.

Among the accompanying papers you will find a copy of the general instructions issued in relation to piracy and the slave trade; they may be found applicable to cases which may arise within the range of your command, although specially designed for another station.

Misrepresentations, arising, no doubt, in most instances, from misapprehension and partial information, have often found their way to the public papers, to the injury of the service and the prejudice of our government. This renders it proper that you should endeavor to prevent communications, from those under your command, respecting the movements of the squadron and your official transactions, which may possibly reach the public in such a manner.

The propriety of such publications must be left to the government, which will take care to afford full information, from the authentic means in its possession, of whatever the interests of the nation will permit to be made known.

You may receive, on board the vessels of your squadron, specie, and the other articles permitted by the act of Congress for the better government of the navy, belonging exclusively to our own citizens, and carry them from one port or place to another, when it does not interfere in any degree with your other more important duties, or infringe the laws of the country where such articles are to be received or carried and, also, on your return to the United Statics, you may bring with you gold, silver, and jewels, the property of our own citizens. But our national vessels ought not, and must not, be used for purposes of commercial adventure; and you are, in no case, to allow anything in the shape of a public advertisement, giving information that you will carry such articles. So many complaints have been made on this subject, that I must impress upon you the necessity of avoiding everything which may give rise to unfriendly comments. In order that the government may be informed of the extent to which the commercial interests of our citizens have been benefitted on this point, and be prepared to answer any inquiries on this subject, you will, from time to time, make reports of all the specie, etc., carried, the places to and from which they may be taken, and the circumstances and conditions under which you do it.

The health of your officers and crew will demand unceasing attention; the moral conduct and professional acquirements of the junior officers, the exercise of constant watchfulness.

Rigid discipline, exactly enforced, is essential to maintain the reputation of the navy, and it must not for one moment be neglected. You are perfectly aware that a firm and energetic course on the part of the superior, accompanied by mild, humane, and gentlemanly deportment, is the best mode of accomplishing, in a satisfactory manner, the various objects entrusted to your command.

On suitable occasions, you will enjoin it upon all grades of officers that they are not to speak reproachfully or contemptuously of each other, disrespectfully of their superiors, nor relate anecdotes, which do no ci-edit to the individual members of the profession nor to the character of the service.

Impress upon them that they are never, on any account, to comment on each other in the public papers, but that each is to maintain in himself, and encourage in others, marked respect, the most decorous language, and the strictest propriety of conduct.

Numerous acts, that may be discreditable to the individual and injurious to the reputation of the navy, cannot always be made the subject of court-martial and legal punishment.

By a strict course of discipline on your part, and attention to language and conduct on that of the officers, it is hoped that there will be less cause for public trials, which have been so numerous as to lessen, in some measure, the warm attachment of the people for the navy.

It has happened that officers on distant stations have been arrested by their commanders, and sent home to await the return of the ships to which they were attached and the officers with whom they have boon associated, thereby creating great expense and inconvenience to the individuals and the service.

I trust that you will be able to maintain proper discipline without a resort to this expedient, which is only to be used when it becomes absolutely necessary.

The midshipmen of the squadron are to objects of unremitted solicitude and care, both as regards their conduct and attainments. Of the common difficulties into which they fall, I presume you are perfectly aware, and they need not be mentioned; but there is one which I fear is not generally known to the commanders, and which, it is said, is frequently practiced to such an extent as to have become an evil; I refer to the habit of borrowing money, articles of dress of all kinds, etc.: it is a habit which produces improvidence and uncleanliness, and ought to be repressed, so far as it can be done in the proper exercise of authority and advice.

It is also especially necessary that commanding officers should guard against the influence of feelings of partiality or prejudice in the treatment of inferiors. Every officer is entitled to, and must enjoy, all the privileges of rank and station. Whenever these are permitted to one and denied to another, or preferences are shown, insubordination and unkind feelings are immediately engendered, to the lasting injury of the service.

I am well persuaded that you do not require to be urged upon this subject, and shall not, therefore, press it further upon your attention.

You will transmit, semi-annually, on the first of January and July, confidential reports of the character, conduct, skill, and acquirements of all the officers under your command. In making them, it is proper that strict impartiality should be used, and all personal prejudices or predilections avoided.

The blank monthly returns, forwarded to you herewith for the use of the squadron, are to be regularly and carefully filled up, and transmitted through you to this Department. The books ordered to be purchased for the use of all our ships in commission are to be placed in charge of the schoolmaster, and on your return carefully packed in boxes, which must be labeled, and deposited in the public store.

It is intended to send out, from time to time, ample supplies for the squadron, which will render it unnecessary for the purser, acting as agent for the squadron, to make purchases, unless on urgent occasions, when special instructions shall be given by you to him.

You will obtain from this officer the funds required for the pay of the officers and men, and the general uses of the squadron; and, to enable him to be at all times ready to meet those demands and fulfill the injunctions of the Department, you will furnish him, from time to time, with estimates in detail of the wants of the squadron, six months in advance, particularizing the various heads of appropriation under which the money should be drawn, and forward the duplicates thereof to this Department.

It may be in your power, while protecting the commercial, to add something to the agricultural interests of our country, by obtaining information respecting valuable animals, seeds, plants, etc.; and by importing such as you can, conveniently, without expense to the government, or neglecting the more immediate and appropriate duties assigned you.

The cultivation of the sugar cane has become an object of increasing importance and value; and you may be able to meet with different varieties in the course of your cruise, and procure directions as to the mode of culture. It is very desirable that this branch of agriculture should not be lost sight of in your inquiries.

The copy of a resolution of Congress, of the twenty-fifth of January, eighteen hundred and thirty, upon this subject, and the collection of vegetables, grain, etc., is enclosed for your information and attention.

There are many scientific, botanical, and agricultural institutions, to which your collections might be profitably entrusted, and by which, whatever you procure, would be applied to the greatest advantage; among them is the Columbian Institute of the city of Washington.

This society, as well as the Treasury Department, has prepared directions for the preservation of articles, and requested that they might be distributed among our naval commanders. In compliance with their wishes, I send you a few copies.

You will make no acting appointments of any description, except in cases of absolute necessity, and then with the express understanding that the appointment ceases with the necessity which called for it; and also taking care to have the same entered upon the muster rolls and proper books of the ships.

As frequently as opportunities offer you will report your proceedings to the Department, transmitting copies of your official correspondence with the authorities of Chili and Peru, and with other powers and persons, and carefully numbering your dispatches, of which it would be prudent to send duplicates by different conveyances.

You will also be the medium of communication to the Department from the officers and men under your command.

Previously to sailing from the United States, you will cause complete muster rolls of all persons on board of the Potomac to be made out and forwarded to the Department.

I am, respectfully, sir, your obedient servant,
LEVI WOODBURY.

Navy Department, July 25, 1831.

MESSRS. NATHANIEL SILSBEE, DUDLEY S. PECKMAN, AND ROBERT STONE:

Gentlemen: Your communication to the President, of the 20th instant, has this day been received and referred to this Department.

I feel happy in assuring you that, since the 19th instant, every necessary preparation has been making to demand immediate redress for the outrage committed.

On the 22d instant, not hearing from Salem but through the newspapers, I addressed a letter to one of your number, as a personal friend, asking further information on this subject, and which letter, were the arrival of this, will doubtless have been received by him. Though it was then confidential, lie is hereby authorized to communicate it to the parties interested.

The Department would now invite attention to procuring and forwarding here a few particulars not contained in the communication received today.

1st. It is desirable to have the originals or authenticated copies of all protests made in relation to the loss, and of affidavits by any persons who witnessed the outrage, detailing its origin and progress.

2d. Any special information as to the character of the rulers and the population, and the part of the country where the injury occurred, which the owners may have, and which is not to be found in the books treating of 'those regions, would be acceptable.

3d. Intelligence is asked as to the political relations, if any, existing between those rulers, etc., and the English or the Dutch; whether useful hints can be given as to the draft of water, dangerous reefs, or circumstances connected with the navigation in that region, and thence to Macao, by a frigate of the largest class.

Your early attention to these subjects will greatly oblige the Department.

With sentiments of respect, I am, gentlemen, your obedient servant, LEVI WOODBURY.

Navy Department, August 9, 1831.

To COMMODORE JOHN DOWNES, OF THE FRIGATE POTOMAC:

Sir: Circumstances have occurred, since the last instructions to you, which require a change in your route to the Pacific, and which may impose on you some new duties, of a character highly delicate and important. A most wanton outrage was committed on the lives and property of certain American citizens at Quallah Batoo, a place on the western side of the Island of Sumatra, on the 7th of February last, the particulars of which are contained in the document annexed, marked A.

You are, therefore, directed to repair at once to Sumatra, by the way of the Cape of Good Hope touching, on the way thither, only at such places as the convenience and necessities of your vessel may render proper. On your arrival at Quallah Batoo, you will obtain from the intelligent shipmasters, supercargoes, and others, engaged in the American trade in that neighborhood, such information as they possess in respect to the nature of the government there, the piratical character of the population and the flagrant circumstances of the injury before mentioned. Should the information substantially correspond with what is given to you in the documents marked A and B, the President of the United States, in order that prompt redress may be obtained for these wrongs, or the guilty perpetrators made to feel that the flag of the Union is not to be insulted with impunity, directs that you proceed to demand of the rajah, or other authorities at Quallah Batoo, restitution of the property plundered, or indemnity therefor, as well as for the injury done to the vessel, satisfaction for any other depredations committed there on our commerce, and the immediate punishment of those concerned in the murder of the American citizens Charles Knight, chief officer, and John Davis and George Chester, seamen, of the ship Friendship.

If a compliance of this demand be delayed beyond a reasonable time, you are authorized, in the following manner, to vindicate our wrongs: Firstly having taken precautions, while making the demand, to cut off all opportunity for escape for individuals either concerned in that savage outrage, or protecting the offenders or participating in the plunder, you will proceed to seize the actual murderers, if they are known, and send them hither for trial as pirates by the first convenient opportunity; to retake such part of the stolen property as can there be found and identified; to destroy the boats and vessels of any kind engaged in the piracy, and the forts and dwellings near the scene of aggression, used for shelter or defense; and to give public information to the population there collected, that if full restitution is not speedily made, and forbearance exercised hereafter from like piracies and murders upon American citizens, other ships-of-war will soon be dispatched thither, to inflict more ample punishment.

Any property restored, or indemnity given, you will deliver to the owners of the ship *Friendship* or their agents, taking receipts therefor. Should the information obtained on the spot give a different character to the transaction from that furnished by the Department, marked A and B, showing any real disapprobation of the plunder and murder by the population at large, or by their rulers, or any provocation given on the part of our citizens, or the existence of a regular, responsible government, acting on principles recognized by civilized nations in their conduct towards strangers, you will confine your operations to a regular demand for satisfaction on the existing authorities at Quallah Batoo, to be rendered by a restoration of the property, indemnity for the other injuries, and a punishment of the offenders. If referred by them to the King of Acheen, you will cause a like demand to be made on him. Should such satisfaction be not speedily given by either, you will inform them that future measures will be taken by the United States effectually to enforce it, and to vindicate the violated rights of their citizens.

At the same time, in this latter event, assure the rajah, or other responsible authorities, that this government entertains no hostile feelings towards the people of Quallah Batoo, or their governors, rajahs, or rulers of any kind; and if the assaults, plundering and murders were unauthorized, and not afterward countenanced, that it will be peculiarly gratifying to discover, on the part of the authorities of those places, a disposition to redress, as far as may be in their power, the wrongs wantonly inflicted on the citizens of the United States.

You will forthwith report to the Department the results of your expedition to Sumatra, forwarding the report by the first convenient opportunity, from that island, or from China.

Leaving Quallah Batoo, or the dominions of the King of Acheen, you will proceed to Macao, where disturbances to our commerce are said to have recently occurred, touching at Batavia, if convenient, and at all events, conferring with our consul there, in person or by letter, on the interests and condition of American commerce in that quarter. To our consul resident in Macao or Canton, and to the American merchants there, you will apply for information, and given any temporary aid or relief in your power, without involving this country in any hostilities with the regular and authorized authorities of China.

After a short stay there for the above objects, and for taking in necessary supplies and refreshments, to obtain which, if indispensable, in addition to the funds placed in your hands already, you are empowered to draw on this Department to the amount of five thousand dollars, you will proceed directly to your station in the Pacific, stopping only at such islands in your way as may be in the usual track, and interesting to our commerce in that region of the world.

Your former instructions will be your guide, after reaching the rest of your squadron; except that whenever a vessel can be spared from it to visit any of the islands in the Pacific, resorted to by our merchantmen and whalers, you are directed to detach one for that purpose.

Great care must be taken to have such vessel conduct with caution, forbearance and good faith towards the natives: to render any assistance in its power to American citizens; to make as favorable an impression as possilble; on the population, of the justice and strength of our government; and to collect and report to this Department all valuable information of every kind connected with the places visited.
With much consideration, your obedient servant,
LEVI WOODBURY

A.
Captain Endicott's statement.

On the 7th of February last, while the Friendship was lying at Quallah Batoo, loading, the captain, two officers, and four of the crew on shore, weighing pepper, she was risen upon by the crew of a Malay pepper boat, who were permitted, contrary to the regulations of the ship, to come on board; and, after killing the first officer, Mr. Charles Knight, of Salem, and two seamen, and badly wounding several others, succeeded in cutting off the ship and plundering her of all the specie on board, amounting to about $12,000, and twelve chests of opium, together with all the ship's papers, spare sails, rigging, cabinet furniture, chronometers, nautical instruments, books, charts, wearing apparel, and, in fact, of every movable article of value on board.

Capt. Endicott with the boat's crew on shore had a narrow escape for their lives. After plundering the ship, the Malays made ineffectual attempts to run her on shore, but by the prompt and timely assistance of the ship *James Munroe*, Porter, of New York, brigs *Gov. Endicott*, H. H. Jenks, of Salem, and *Palmer*, Powers, of Boston, the ship was retaken before they could accomplish their object. The particulars, as taken from the ship's log book, after the accident, are as follows:

Monday, February 7, 1831.

"At eight o'clock, A. M., the captain, two officers, and four men went on shore to weigh pepper; at half-past three, P. M., succeeded in procuring one boat load; saw her leave the bank of the river, opposite the scale house, with the usual complement of men in her, that is to say, one steersman and six oarsmen; the natives still bringing pepper to the scales, with the promise of giving us another boat load today. The first boat was observed to make considerable delay in getting out of the river, and we supposed her crew might be stealing pepper from her, and secreting it among the neighboring high grass. Two of the ship's men were accordingly sent down to watch them, and, upon their approaching the boat, five or six Malays were seen to jump up from the grass and hurry on board her; the ship's people supposed them to be the boat's crew, as they had seen about the same number quit her previous to their being observed by the Malays. At this time, there was a brig standing into Soo-Soo. While waiting for the natives to complete our other boat load of pepper. Captain Endicott went to the beach to ascertain if the brig approaching had hoisted any colors. He then saw that the pepper boat, which, at this time, was within a few yards of the ship, had at least double the number of men in her that she had when she left the scales. He immediately returned, and inquired into this circumstance. The men who were sent down to watch the boat in the river then informed him that they had seen her take in several men out of a ferry boat, at the mouth of the river; but, as they all appeared to be "youngsters," they did not think the circumstance of sufficient importance to report it. Our suspicions were immediately excited that all was not right; yet, trusting they would not be permitted to go on board, it being contrary to the established regulations of the ship, in the absence of the captain, to admit more than two Malays on board her at a time and deeming it too late to render any assistance if they were, the second officer and two men were sent to the beach to observe the movements on board, who almost instantly returned with the information that there was trouble on board, and that men were seen jumping overboard from her. Convinced from this circumstance that we on shore had no time to lose, we immediately sprang into the ship's boat, and pushed off. Almost instantaneously crowds of Malays began to assemble on the banks of the river, which are about sixty yards asunder, brandishing their weapons, and otherwise menacing us; at the same moment, a ferry boat, with eight or ten men in her, armed with spears and knives, pushed off to intercept our passage out of the river; but by pulling directly for her, and presenting — a Malay sword, our only weapon, we succeeded in keeping them off. When we cleared the river, and came in full sight of the ship, we found the Malays had full possession of her, some of them walking about the deck, while others were making signals of success to the people on shore; none of the ship's crew, except one man aloft, was to be seen. At this moment, three Malay boats, with forty or fifty men each, came out of the river and pulled towards the ship and us. We then concluded our only chance to recover the ship was by obtaining assistance from some other vessel; and for this purpose we made the best of our way to Muckie, where we knew two or three American vessels were lying. At one A. M., we reached Muckie, which lies twenty-five miles distant from Quallah Batoo, and found there ship *James Monroe*, Porter, of New York; brigs *Governor Endicott*, H. H. Jenks, of Salem, and *Palmer*, Powers, of Boston; who determined, on hearing our misfortune, to proceed to Quallah Batoo and endeavor to recover the ship. They accordingly got under way, but, owing to the lightness of the wind, did not reach Quallah Batoo in season to effect anything that day; but, on the morning of the 9th, a Malay was sent on shore to demand the ship of the rajah, accompanied with the threat that, if the Malays did not immediately desert h.er, we should fire upon them and the town. The rajah, however, positively refused to give her up, and sent word we might take her if we could. The three vessels then commenced firing upon the ship and the boats, which were passing with plunder, and were answered by the forts on shore, the Malays also firing the ship's guns at us.

In their attempts to run her on shore she had become entangled among a large cluster of shoals, which rendered it extremely dangerous for either of the vessels to attempt to lay her alongside. The Malays, however, after blowing themselves up with an open keg of powder, out of which they were loading the guns, soon ceased firing on board the ship, when a boat from each vessel was dispatched to board her, under cover of the guns from the vessels, and which we did without opposition; the Malays deserting her on the approach of the boats. We found her within pistol shot of the shore; and, on examination, ascertained that she was plundered of everything valuable, and scarcely anything but her pepper remaining.

"The appearance of the ship, at the time we boarded her, beggars all description; every part of her bore ample testimony of the scene of violence and destruction with which she had been visited. We subsequently learned that the pepper boat exchanged her crew of fishermen, at the river's mouth, for a set of opium smokers, rendered desperate by their habits, and to these men added, also, others of the same class, taken from the ferry boat; that, when she came alongside, not one of them was recognized by the ship's company as having been off to her before. They were all, however, indiscriminately permitted to go on board, and the attack was commenced simultaneously at different parts of the ship, by some concerted signal. Three or four men, with the first officer, were instantly krised; and the crew, being taken by surprise, and unprepared, the ship fell an easy prey to them.

"Killed on board the Friendship: Mr. Charles Wright, chief officer; John Davis and George Chester seamen. Wounded: Charles Converse, seaman, badly; John Massey, seaman, and William Francis steward."

Further particulars:

Captain Endicott informs us, in addition to the particulars before given, that just as he had pushed off from the shore, at Quallah Batoo, half the boat's length, (after learning his ship had been attacked) Po Adam, a jerretoolis, (clerk,) formerly of Quallah Batoo, but for the last two or three years a resident of Pulo Kio a man of considerable property and influence, sprang into the boat, bringing with him his sword and other arms. Captain Endicott said to him, at the moment of his reaching the boat

"What, do you come too, Adam?" "Yes," was his answer; "if they kill you they must kill me first captain." to this man, Captain Endicott and the boat's crew felt that they principally owed, under Providence, their escape; as the appearance of his weapons, no doubt, gave the Malays in the ferry boat the impression that all on board the Friendship's boat were armed, and they in consequence suffered the latter to pass almost without molestation.

After having thus cleared the river, Captain Endicott submitted himself much to the counsel and advice of Adam; and when he concluded to proceed with all dispatch to Muckie for assistance, this man not only piloted the boat in the night, but pulled an oar nearly the whole distance; and discovered as much anxiety that every possible dispatch should be made in' procuring assistance, as if he was to be personally benefited by the recapture of the ship. To his exertions, Captain Endicott also owed the recovery of some of his nautical instruments. For the interest Po Adam took in this affair, the Malays at Quallah Batoo confiscated all his property which they could get hold of at that place, amounting to several thousand dollars and even set a price upon his life. The conduct of this generous and noble-hearted Malay should entitle him to the gratitude of every American, and we hope he will not go unrewarded. Four of the Friendship's crew, who jumped overboard at the time of the attack, swam the distance of two miles before they could find a safe place to land, as the Malays lined the shore for some distance around Quallah Batoo. As soon as they reached the shore they fled into the bushes; where, almost without clothing, and having nothing to subsist on, they remained for three days — at night walking to and fro in hopes of finding some means of escape. The third night they discovered a canoe, which they took possession of, and proceeded for Pulo Kio, the residence of Po Adam, knowing that they would be safe if they put themselves under his protection. On their arrival they were informed of the recapture of the ship; and the benevolent Adam not only furnished them with clothing, but, with two of his men, proceeded with them himself in their canoe, and put them on board the ship *James Monroe* of New York.

At the time of the attack upon the crew of *the Friendship*, Mr. Knight, the chief mate, was busily engaged in taking an account of pepper. The Malays had placed themselves in the best manner for making the attack. All the men who were killed or wounded, (seven in number) were struck at the same moment. Two of the Malays stabbed Mr. Knight, one at his side and the other at his back. He ran to the starboard side of the quarter-deck and seized a boarding pike, after he was wounded he was there met by one of the ship's crew, who heard him exclaim, "Do your duty." He was immediately after seen lying dead near the same place, with the boarding pike under him, the Malays having rushed upon and dispatched him.

The exultation of the natives at this achievement was unbounded, and their insolence insufferable. When Captain Endicott, and the other American masters and supercargoes, landed at South Tallapow after the recapture of the ship, the natives followed them through the streets iu great crowds, exulting and hooting, with exclamations suitable to these: "Who great man now, Malay or American?" "How many man American dead?" "How many man Malay dead?" etc. What the consequence of such a feeling will be, it is impossible to foretell. May the mistake under which they rest, that the Americans have not the power to chastise them, be corrected with all convenient dispatch!

AMOUNT OF INJURY.

Specie [1]	$12,536 00
Opium	$8,180 00
Stores and provisions	$2,500 00
Instruments and clothes	$1,200 00
Loss of voyage, freight, etc.	$14,000 00
Salvage, etc.	$9,000 00

The attack was evidently concerted some time beforehand, and one of the acting rajahs aided in the combination. The Achenese rajah, Chute Dulah, received the specie and opium into his possession, and refused the restoration of that, as well as of the ship. Others of distinction united, and hired persons of less note to go on board and commit the outrage and murders.

B.

CHARACTER AND CONDITION OF THE POPULATION AND COUNTRY AT QUALLAH BATOO, IN THE ISLAND OF SUMATRA.

Quallah Batoo is situated in about 3 deg. 44 min. north latitude, and 96 deg. 56 min. east longitude, on the western side of the Island of Sumatra.

That part of the island is called the Battas, and is in the possession of the natives, who owe no particular allegiance to any

[1] *Specie: coins or other metal money in mass circulation*

foreign power, and a very slight one, if any, to the King of Acheen, whose country is northwest of the Battas, and who does not hold himself responsible for their outrages.

The different tribes have rajahs, or chiefs, sometimes two each, and often wantonly plunder and kill strangers, without possessing any civilized principles of government conforming to national law, so as to permit or open regular diplomatic relations with the rest of the world. They frequently war with each other, and with the King of Acheen, with much perfidy and barbarity. Neither the British nor Dutch, claim any control over that part of Sumatra; and the nearest fort of the former is at Tappanooly.

Many American vessels resort to that coast, and are in danger of capture, and of having their crews murdered, from the savage and piratical conduct and principles of the population. The arrogance and treachery of the natives, especially towards Americans, have, of late years, increased; and, in this instance, their aggressions were countenanced beforehand by some of those in authority, and all relief and restoration, when demanded were refused.

Quallah Batoo lies entirely open to the sea, defended by only two or three small forts, of three or four guns each, having a nupufation, including the pepper plantations, four or live miles in the interior, of about lour thousand. Tlie depth of water in the roads, within a quarter and half a mile of the shore, is from eighteen to twenty fathoms - muddy bottom; but much stone, flung in from ballast, rendering chain cables expedient when at anchor.

U. S. FRIGATE POTOMAC, off Soo-Soo, Coast of Sumatra, February 11, 1832.

Sir: I have the honor to acquaint you with the arrival of *the Potomac* on this coast upon the 5th instant. I anchored off Quallah Batoo, distant about three miles, my object in doing so being to prevent a discovery of the character of the ship, which I had previously taken care to disguise; and so effectively that a number of fishermen, who came on board after I had anchored, did not discover that she was other than a merchant ship until they came over the side. They were detained on board till after the capture of Quallah Batoo.

Finding no vessels on the coast, I could obtain no information, in addition to that already possessed, respecting the nature of the government, the piratical character of the population, or the flagrant circumstances of the injury done to *the Friendship*.

No demand of satisfaction was made previous to my attack, because I was satisfied, from what knowledge I had already of the character of the people, that no such demand would be answered, except only by refusal, and that such refusal would proceed from want of ability, as well as of inclination, it being a habit generally among this people to spend their money as soon as obtained.

Soon after anchoring, Lieutenants Shubrick, Pinkham, Hoff, Ingersoll and Edson, of the marines, together with Passed Midshipmen Totten and Tooley, went on shore in the whale boat, for the purpose of learning the situation of the town and forts; but everything being built in close concealment, they were unable to arrive at any satisfactory result, except as to one of the forts, erected immediately at the place of landing.

No precautions were taken to cut off the opportunity of escape from any of the inhabitants of the town, the nature of the place rendering it absolutely impossible, situated as it is, in the midst of wood and jungle, impenetrable except by private passages, known only to the natives.

As soon as it became sufficiently dark to prevent our movements from discovery by the people on shore, the boats were hoisted out, and every preparation was made for the landing, which was effected about daybreak of the 6th inst. The party under command of Lieutenant Shubrick consisted of two hundred and fifty men.

I adopted this mode of enforcing our demands, in hopes of getting possession of the persons of the rajahs, by surrounding and surprising the forts in which they usually reside, and thus most probably inducing the payment of money for their ransoms. I regret to say, however, that in consequence of their desperate fighting, neither giving nor receiving quarter, no prisoners were made, nor was any property found belonging to *the Friendship*, save the medicine chest.

Lieutenant Shubrick has my warmest acknowledgments for the able and gallant manner in which he conducted the expedition, and I enclose herewith that gentleman's report, wherein he gives a detailed account of the attack, together with other particulars.

The midshipmen who were on shore, and engaged in the action, but not named by Lieutenant Shubrick, were William May, in the first division, under Lieutenant Pinkham; Messrs. Alonzo B. Davis, James G. Stanley and Charles W. Morris, of the second division, commanded by Lieutenant Hoff; and of the third division, under the command of Lieutenant Ingersoll, Messrs. Charles Hunter, Eugene Boyle and James L. Parker, with Midshipman George T. Sinclair in the launch.

Their gallantry and good conduct in the action are spoken of as deserving the highest praise.

In consequence of the fort (situated south of the river,) having fired upon our men while attacking Quallah Batoo, I ran in with the ship, and fired about three broadsides into it, when a white flag was hoisted. Upon this I ceased firing; soon after got under way and stood for this anchorage, where I am taking on board wood and water.

While lying here, a flag of truce has been sent off from Quallah Batoo, and I was informed by the hearer of the same that a great many had been killed on shore, and that all the property there was destroyed. He begged that I would grant them peace. I stated to him that I had been sent here to demand restitution of the property taken from the Friendship, and to insist on the punishment of those persons who were concerned in the outrage committed on the individuals of that ship.

Finding it impossible to effect either object, I said to him that I was satisfied with what had already been done, and I granted them the peace for which they begged. I at the same time assured him that if forbearance should not be exercised hereafter from committing piracies and murders upon American citizens, other ships-of-war would be dispatched to inflict upon them further punishment.

Several rajahs from towns in this vicinity have visited my ship, and others who are distant have sent deputations to me. All of them have declared their friendly disposition towards the Americans, and their desire to obtain our friendship. Corresponding assurances were given on my part, and they left the ship apparently well satisfied.

Having obtained wood and water, and refreshed my crew, I shall leave here tomorrow for Batavia.

I have the honor to be, very respectfully, your obedient servant.
JNO. DOWNES.

U. S. Ship Potomac, of the Town of Quallah Batoo,
February 6, 1832.

Hon. Levi Woodbury, Secretary of the Navy, Washington City.

Sir: I have the honor to inform you that, according to your orders heretofore received, I effected a landing, with the several divisions under my command, about one mile and a half to the northward of the town. Although there was a heavy surf upon the shore, the divisions were landed and formed without the slightest accident. The following, was the order observed. First, the marines under Lieutenant Edson, then the different divisions under the command of Lieutenants Pinkham, Hoff, and Ingersoll and the six pounder in charge of Acting Sailingmaster Totten; the boats being left in the command of Passed Midshipmen Godon, with order to follow to the town as soon as the attack commenced. I feel much indebted to Lieutenants Edson and Terrett for the promptness displayed by them in forming the marines, and assisting and forming the other divisions: all of which was effected with coolness in fifteen minutes. As soon as the day dawned, we proceeded along the beach towards the town, undiscovered by the enemy until within a short distance of the northernmost fort, when I immediately dispatched Lieutenant Hoff with his division to surround it, and, in the event and the enemies firing upon him, to carry it by storm. As soon as he approached the gateway, he was fired on, when after a close action of nearly two hours, the American flag was hoisted, the enemy carrying off this wounded, and leaving behind him his dead, twelve in number, and the women. Lieutenant Hoff had to surmount great difficulties in the capture of the fort, he tore up the palisades that surrounded it, and formed another bridge, upon which he entered, and drove the enemy from their almost impregnable position; during the whole of which time an incessant fire was kept up on him.

After leaving Lieutenant Hoff, I proceeded with the remaining forces, and, at the northern end of the town, Lieutenants Pinkham and Edson, with their respective divisions, filed off to the left, to the attack of the two forts assigned to them, in the rear of the town; while, with the third division under Lieutenant Ingersoll, and the six-pounder in charge of Acting Sailingmaster Totten, I pushed on to attach the principal and strongest fort, situated at the southern end of the town. At the distance of fifty yards from the fort, perceiving the enemy preparing to receive us, I directed the six-pounder loaded with round and grape, to be discharged which threw them into confusion. The coolness and precision Acting Sailingmaster Totten worked the six-pounder, did great execution during the action. Lieutenant Ingersoll at this time rush on to the attack. At this juncture Lieutenant Pinkham, with the first division rejoined me; Sailingmaster Barry, the guide, having been unable from the material alterations in and around the fort, assigned to Lieutenant Pinkham, to point it out. The pioneers, with their crows and axes, having forced the gate, portions of the first and third divisions, under the direction of their respective officers, rushed into the area, and took possession with little resistance, but few Malays appearing, two of whom were killed on the spot. A charge was then made at the inner gate, which communicated with a narrow passage leading to the stronghold of the enemy (which was a strong platform, considerably elevated, upon which were mounted several cannon protected by a thick wall), which being forced it was discovered, to the disappointment of the officers and the men there engaged, that the ladder leading to the platform had been drawn up, and in an effectual attempt to climb the parapet, I regret to say that William R. Smith, seaman was killed; Henry Dutcher, ordinary seaman, and Levi McCabe, quarter-gunner, of the third division were wounded, and Midshipman J.W. Taylor, and Peter Walsh, ordinary seamen of the first division were also wounded. I then gave the order to fire the buildings within the area, which was promptly done, but it being calm, and these buildings being detached from the main fort, the fire did not communicate with it as I had hoped. A short time after the fire commenced, two magazines blew up, but I am happy to state that the explosion injured none of us, although in their immediate neighborhood. Lieutenants Hoff and Edson, after storming the forts after which they had been sent, hoisted the American flag and leaving a detachment in each, they formed between the fort and water, thus a brisk fire was thus poured in from two sides. Passed Midshipman Godon, in the launch, took a position immediately in front of the fort, and kept-up a spirited and well-directed fire, but so tenaciously did the enemy cling to their position, that not until nearly all of them had been destroyed could we carry the fort. This was however, gallantly done by Lieutenant Ingersoll, Pass Midshipman Sylvanus Godon, and Midshipmen Joseph C. Walsh, J. W. Taylor, and Henry D. Hart, who spiked and threw the guns from the platform. The American colors where then hoisted, with three hearty cheers. Apprehending that the enemy had lain a train to his magazine, and the fort being mostly destroyed and completely dismantled, I deemed it proper to call off the officers and men, as it would have been an act of inhumanity to expose them to explosion.

 For some time previous to the surrender of this last fort, another situated about one hundred and fifty yards from the east bank of the river, and upon the opposite side of it, had been firing upon us with a twelve pounder. It being impracticable to enter the river with our boats, and not possible to ford it without wetting our firearms, I did not deem it expedient to attack this, but made preparations for the reduction of another in the neighborhood of the one left in charge of Lieutenant Terrett of the marines, which would have remained undiscovered, (the town and forts being situated in so thick a jungle), had the enemy not opened fire upon Lieutenant Terrett. I immediately dispatched Lieutenants Pinkham and Edson, with portions of their divisions, to reduce it; when, being invested on two sides, the enemy, after a short but ferocious resistance, fled to the jungle with much loss. It pains me, sir, to state, with this attack, private Benjamin T. Brown was killed, and private Daniel H. Cole wounded, supposed mortally. I omitted to mention, in its proper place, that John L. Dubois, seaman, belonging to Lieutenant Hoff's division, was severely wounded by a saber cut on the head and hand, and several others slightly, from darts and javelins. The action having lasted nearly two hours and a half, and the town being almost reduced to ashes, the surf at same time rising very fast, I deemed it prudent to commence the embarkation, under cover of the marines, hoping that what had been done would meet with your approbation.

From the knowledge of the place possessed by Sailingmaster Barry, and his coolness, I derived the utmost advantage. Assistant Surgeons Foltz and Pawling were active and zealous in the discharge of their duties, binding up and dressing the wounded under the fire of the enemy. The different orders I had occasion to send to those separated from me, were conveyed with promptness and great precision by Passed Midshipman Tooley and Purser William A. Slacum. The lieutenants commanding the different divisions have reported to me the entire satisfaction they derived from the coolness and bravery of the officers and men under their particular commands. I feel it a duty to state to you how much I am indebted to Lieutenants Pinkham, Hoff, Ingersoll, and Edson, for the promptness and alacrity with which they executed all orders, and my warm admiration for the gallantry evinced by them upon all occasions. The loss of the enemy must have been considerable; at least one hundred and fifty killed. I am happy to state that among the killed, were Poolow N. Yamet, commonly called Po Mahomet, the principle rajah, concerned with the plunder and massacre of the crew of *the Friendship*. We captured one pair of colors, twenty-six, stand of arms, and one brass field-piece. We also set fire and destroyed a number of proas on the stocks. The cannon in all the forts, with the exception of one, being of iron, were spiked and thrown over the parapet, the powder destroyed. The following is a list of the killed and wounded:

Killed: William P. Smith, seaman; Benjamin T. Brown, marine.

Wounded: Lieutenant Edson, contused leg; Midshipman J. W. Taylor, slightly; Daniel H. Cole, marine, supposed mortally; Henry Dutcher (O. S.), severely; Peter Walsh (O. S.), severely; Levi M'Cabe (qr. gun.), slightly; John L. Dubois, seaman, severely; John Addison, seaman, slightly; James G. Huster, marine, slightly; James P. Noland (O. S.), slightly; James McCabe (O. S.) slightly.

I have the honor to be, sir, very respectfully, your obedient servant, IRVINE SHUBRICK, Lieut, commanding the Expedition.

INDEX

A

Acheen, Sumatra 9, 11, 12
Adam, Po
  16, 18, 20, 23, 32, 33, 40, 41, 59
Addison, John, seaman 68
Annalaboo, Sumatra 31, 32

B

Barry, John, second mate
  13, 18, 19, 20, 21, 23, 39
Barry, Sailingmaster, USS Potomac
  67
Batavia 64
de Bieulieu, Commodore Antoine
  Georges N. 11, 12, 41
Boston, Mass. 56, 57
Boyle, Eugene 64
Bray, William, carpenter 13, 29
Brown, Benjamin, marine 67, 68
Bryne, John, crewmember 13

C

Canton, China 55
Cape Felix, Sumatra 31, 32
Cape of Good Hope 53
Chester, George, seaman
  13, 30, 53, 59
Chute Dulah 61
Cole, Daniel H., marine 67, 68
Collins, George, seaman 13
Columbian Institute 51
Converse, Charles, seaman
  13, 34, 59

D

Davis, Alonzo B. 64

Davis, John, seaman
  13, 34, 35, 53, 59
the Delphos 38
the Dolphin 46
Downes, John, Com. 39, 45, 64
Dubois, John L., Seaman 67, 68
Dutcher, Henry, Ordinary Seaman
  66, 68

E

East India Company 11, 12
Edson, Lieutenant 63, 65, 66, 67, 68
Queen Elizabeth I 12
Endicott, Charles 55, 56, 59, 60

F

the Fair American 35
the Falmouth 46
Folyz, Assistant Surgeon 67
Francis, William, steward 13, 34, 59

G

Gillie, Capt. James D. of the Delphos
  38
Godon, Passed Midshipmen 65, 66
the Gov. Endicott
  24, 37, 38, 56, 57, 24, 25
Gregory, Master Commandant 46

H

Hammond, Capt. of the *ship Maria*, of
  New York 42, 43
Hart, Henry, Midshipman 66
Hoff, Lieutenant 63, 64, 65, 66, 67
Hunter, Charles 64
Huster, James G., marine 68

I

Ingersoll, Lieutenant
  63, 64, 65, 66, 67

J

Jackson, Andrew 45
the James Monroe
   25, 27, 29, 33, 56, 57, 60
Jenks, H.H., Capt. of the Gov.
   Endicott 24, 38, 56, 57

K

King of Acheen 54, 62
Knight, Charles, first mate
   13, 16, 18, 30, 53, 55, 60

L

Long, Lt. John C. 46

M

Macao 52, 54
Mahomet, Po 67
Manning, Philip, seaman 13, 19
Massey, John, seaman
   13, 29, 35, 59
May, William 64
McCabe, James, Ordinary Seaman
   68
McCabe, Levi, Ordinary Seaman
   66, 68
Migell, Lorenzo, cook 13, 34
Morris, Charles W. 64
Muckie, Sumatra 57

N

New York, New York 46, 56, 57
Noland, James P., Ordinary Seaman
   68
Norfolk, Virginia 46

P

the Palmer 24, 25, 56, 57
Parker, James L. 64
Parnell, William, seaman
   13, 29, 30, 31

Patterson, John, seaman 13
Pawling, Assistant Surgeon 67
Peabody, Joseph Esq. of Salem, Mass.
   42
Peckman, Dudley S. 52
Pedechio, Gregorie, seaman
   13, 34, 35, 37
Pedir Coast 13
Pedir Rajah 14
Pernambuco, St. Salvador 46
Phoenicians 9
Pickman, Dudley Leavitt (1779-1846)
   13
Pinkham, Lieutenant
   63, 64, 65, 66, 67
Plymouth, Mass. 12
Porter, Capt. of the James Monroe
   56, 57
Porto Praya, Cape Verde Islands 46
Powers, Capt. of the Palmer
   24, 56, 57
Pulo Kio, Sumatra
   13, 16, 29, 32, 33, 38, 41, 59

Q

Quallah Batoo, Sumatra 13, 14, 15,
   24, 25, 31, 32, 33, 36,
   39, 42, 45, 53, 54, 55,
   57, 58, 59, 60, 61, 62,
   64, 65
Quallah, Po 14

R

Rio de Janeiro, Brazil 46

S

Salem, Mass. 13, 52, 56, 57
Shubrick, Irvine, Lt. 63, 64, 68
Silsbee, Nathaniel 13, 52
Sinclair, George T., Midshipman 64
Slacum, William A. Purser 67
Smith, William R., Seaman 66, 68

South Tallapow, Sumatra 38
Stanley, James G. 64
Stone, Robert 52

T

Taylor, J.W., Midshipman 66, 68
Terrett, Lieutenant 65, 67
Tooley, Passed Midshipman 63, 67
Totten, Acting Sailingmaster 63, 65

U

US Potomac, Frigate 39, 40

V

Van Buren, Martin 46

W

Walsh, Joseph C., Midshipman 66
Walsh, Peter, Ordinary Seaman
    66, 68
Warren, Algernon, seaman 13, 29
Washington, D.C. 51
West Indies 48
Woodbury, Levi 52, 65

Y

Yamet, Poolow N. 67